I have watercress!

arugula!

radishes!

zuchini!

string beans!

escarolle!

from BALDUCCIS!!!!

and a little cooked baked sweet potatoe from John!
AND NEW CRANBERRY RELISH!
AND ST. ANDRE CHEESE!

Love,

Icebox

Love, Icebox

Letters from John Cage to Merce Cunningham

Foreword, Commentary, and Afterword by Laura Kuhn

For Monique,
a beautiful comrade
in arms!

Laura Kuhn
New York
2019

The John Cage Trust 2019

John Cage Trust
Bard College
1309 Annandale Road
Red Hook, New York 12571
www.johncage.org

Distributed by Artbook/D.A.P.
75 Broad Street, Suite 630
New York, NY 10004
www.artbook.com

Design by Naomi Yang

Front cover loft photo: James Daubney ©James Daubney
Back cover: Cage & Cunningham (from New Dance USA 1981)
Courtesy of the Collection Walker Art Center

Printed in Belgium by die Keure

Contents

Something of the Beginning by Laura Kuhn

John Cage and Merce Cunningham have long been known as a dynamic collaborative duo—in life as in the arts—but it's never been entirely clear just how and when they came together. They first met at the Cornish School in Seattle in the late 1930s, of course, but this was hardly the time or place. Cage was a teacher and Cunningham a student, seven years apart in age, and, in any case, Cage was happily married to his young Alaska-born Russian wife, Xenia (née Kashavaroff). Cage declared his meeting with Xenia love at first sight, and the two eloped to Yuma, Arizona, where they were married on June 7, 1935. (Yuma was the marriage capital of Arizona throughout the 1930s, most likely because the neighboring state of California had a "gin marriage law," which mandated a three-day waiting period so that couples could sober up before tying the knot.) Years later, Cunningham would remember Cage as serious, even formidable. He also recalled that many of his fellow students at Cornish referred to him not by name, but as "the handsome new man in the red sweater."

Cage had joined the faculty to teach, compose, and accompany dance classes, and he often performed with his newly formed percussion ensemble which usually included Xenia Cage, Doris Dennison (the eurhythmics teacher), Margaret Jenkins (another member of the music faculty), and occasionally Cunningham (notably in two programs, given on December 9, 1938, and May

19, 1939). The ensemble gave concerts in Seattle and throughout the Northwest, usually at universities. Cage taught four courses across the 1939 summer sessions: "Modern Dance Composition," "Experimental Music," "Creative Music Education for Teachers," and "Creative Music for Children." He also systematized the prepared piano, for which he composed some early jewels and later became well known, in 1949 garnering an unexpected grant from the Guggenheim Foundation. He also organized what was likely the first program in the U.S. entirely devoted to percussion music, soliciting scores from fellow composers far and wide. And he began composing with electronics, his *Imaginary Landscape No. 1* (1939) calling for the use of variable-speed phonograph turntables playing recordings of static and sliding test tones. It was, as Cage later reflected, "in effect a piece of proto-*musique concrète*." The first performance by John and Xenia Cage, Dennison, and Jenkins took place in two studios, their sounds picked up by two separate microphones and mixed in the control booth in the radio studio of the Cornish School. This was a prescient endeavor in 1939. As Cage's biographer Kenneth Silverman wittily noted in *Begin Again: A Biography of John Cage* (Knopf, 2012): "The acoustic pianist and percussionist at one microphone, the turntable players at another, primitive techno-culture DJs!"

Neither Cage nor Cunningham remained in Seattle for very long. After two years of study, first as a student in the theater department and then in dance, Cunningham was wooed by the doyen of modern dance, Martha Graham, who had seen him perform in a summer program at Mills College and promised him a spot in her company should he find himself in New York. Cunningham's mother wasn't thrilled with the idea, but, as Cunningham recalled, his father was less resistant. "Oh, mother, let him go," he said. "If that kid didn't have that dance game, he'd be a crook." The Cages left the Cornish School not long after, at the end of the spring

semester of 1940, although they remained in California for another year or so before making their way east.

Cage was gaining notoriety on the West Coast and was invited to teach during a summer session or two at Mills College by his good friend, the composer Lou Harrison. One of his earliest programs there, on July 18, 1940, which included works by not only Cage and Harrison but by Henry Cowell, Amadeo Roldán, José Ardévol, and William Russell as well, yielded enthusiastic notices in the *San Francisco Chronicle* and *Time* magazine. In early 1941, Harrison and Cage jointly composed a percussion quartet, *Double Music*, each working independently to produce two of its four parts

(Cage writing for the soprano and tenor instruments, Harrison for the alto and bass). The work premiered at San Francisco's California Club on May 14, 1941, the ensemble performing on a battery of instruments that included bells, brake drums, sistra, gongs, tam-tams, and thunder sheet, most drawn from Cage's own collection. In fact, by the time the Cages had reached Mills College, Cage had amassed some 150 percussion instruments, many quite exotic and including a Léon Theremin-designed Rhythmicon (the first electronic drum "rhythm" machine), which he obtained from his good friend and mentor Henry Cowell, founder of the important publication *New Musical Resources*.

Cage's various musical pursuits of the time came together in his desire to establish a Center for Experimental Music. He worked tirelessly to gather funds and to persuade a variety of individuals and institutions to sponsor it, but his overtures were either turned down or simply ignored. Among those to whom he proposed the Center was the émigré painter and photographer Lászlo Moholy-Nagy. Formerly an influential teacher at the Bauhaus in Germany, Moholy-Nagy had established a sort of American Bauhaus in Chicago, the School of Design. Accepting Moholy-Nagy's invitation to teach there, Cage and his wife moved to Chicago in the fall of 1941. In addition to teaching his course "Sound Experiments" at the School of Design, to make ends meet Cage also taught at the University of Chicago and accompanied dance classes led by Kay Manning. His least favorite job appears to have been as an accompanist for three hours every Thursday evening at Hull House, co-founded in 1889 by Jane Adams and Ellen Gates Starr, a settlement house for the poor and center for social reformers and intelligentsia, John Dewey among its trustees. (Ironically, none other than Pauline Schindler, years earlier Cage's inamorata, had been on the staff of Hull House, from 1917 to 1919.) Perhaps most important, he befriended Rue Shaw, president of the distinguished Arts Club of Chicago. It would be at the Arts Club that Cage would give an even more raucous percussion concert on March 1, 1942, which attracted national attention. An ensemble of nine performers played such unexpected instruments as tin cans, a siren, and even a lime rickey soda bottle, which was shattered by being thrown into a can of broken glass by Xenia Cage at the culmination of her husband's *First Construction (in Metal)* (1939).

Neither Cage nor Xenia cared much for Chicago. The physical appearance of the city was not to their liking ("An Ugly City," Cage once wrote, with "too much soot"), and the school itself was not entirely as expected. He especially bemoaned the lack of discrete classroom space. (This from the composer who some 25 years later would create the *Musicircus*, a musical form in which simultaneity is *de rigueur*.) With benefit of hindsight, however, we now see Chicago as an important way station for Cage for primarily two reasons: the creation and premiere broadcast of his startlingly original radio play *The City Wears a Slouch Hat*, and the resurfacing into the Cages' lives of Merce Cunningham.

The City Wears a Slouch Hat was commissioned by the Columbia Broadcasting System (CBS), its text by the American poet and novelist, Kenneth Patchen. This was to be an experimental program for the popular series known as the "Columbia Workshop" and *The City Wears a Slouch Hat* was given its one and only broadcast over the CBS network on May 31, 1942, from 2:00 to 2:30 p.m. on a Sunday afternoon. The percussion ensemble was conducted by Cage, the players including Cilia Amidon, Xenia Cage, Ruth Hartman, Stuart Lloyd, and Claire Oppenheim. While the broadcast didn't prove to be Cage's ticket to fame or fortune—nor did it allow him to fulfill his dream of composing a fully electronic work by using only the recorded sound effects available at the radio station—it didn't go unnoticed. Letters poured in to both the Chicago and New York CBS stations. Some expressed mild confusion, some extolled the work's virtues, and one went so far as to suggest that the collaborators be committed to an asylum.

Cunningham's reappearance in Cage's life in Chicago was not entirely surprising and very much welcome. Martha Graham and Dance Company gave a program at the Civic Opera House on March 14, 1942, in which Cunningham was featured. One of Cage's earliest letters to Cunningham, dated a week later, is newsy in tone and brimming with enthusiasm. "Nobody recognizes Nijinsky when they see him," says he, softening his report on what were mostly tepid local reviews.

Cage's letters to Cunningham, found among Cunningham's personal effects after his death in 2009, will be revelatory for many. Eleven of these letters appeared in *The Selected Letters of John Cage* (Wesleyan University Press, 2016), but another 28, combined spanning the years 1942 to 1946, will be new to most as they are published here for the first time. Cage shows himself to be an enterprising young musician, brimming with novel ideas and seemingly endless energy and talent. He's also clearly a man who's falling in love. His letters to Cunningham over the ensuing years are increasingly passionate, distraught, romantic, and confused, and occasionally even contain snippets of poetry and song. At the same time, they are more than love letters, since we see intimations of all manner of things that resonate with our experience of the later John Cage: his penchant for making strong and important associations, his musings on the purpose of music and the possibilities in composition, his warm and playful humor and his gift for language, his enthusiastic engagement with community, and even his devotion to the French composer Erik Satie.

Love, Icebox

Wednesday *[postmarked January 14, 1942]*
323 East Cermak Road, Chicago

Dear Merce:

Mrs. Shaw hasn't yet gone to N.Y. I have spoken to her about you
and Jean and will again at the last minute before she goes. I would
have written to you about her not leaving to N.Y. yet, except that
I am gradually going crazy with concert rehearsals etc. I think
the important thing is to go on working and not have a feeling
of waiting. I will write again the day I know definitely that she is
leaving for N.Y.

     Yours,
     John

Although Cunningham's letters to Cage from this period
have yet to surface, the two men had obviously been in touch.
We can assume from this short letter that Cunningham had
asked Cage for an introduction to Rue Shaw, President of the
Arts Club of Chicago, perhaps to take place in person during
one of her upcoming trips to New York.

[Undated, postmarked March 21, 1942]
323 East Cermak Road, Chicago

Dear Merce:

This is very tardy in comparison with telegrams, menus, etc. It is because we were completely sad that the reviews were impossible to send. Bulliet hated it. Smith stayed only for the first dance, didn't like it. And nobody liked it who got into print. It wasn't the truth, but we couldn't send reviews. If you still want them, let us know again, and we will blindfold ourselves.

Martha's new dance seemed very good to me, although it was obviously ballet form, war-horse form; but I enjoyed it. One thing, the space of that stage is magnificent. And you were marvelous, and it was good to see the group moving around. Nobody liked Eric[k Hawkins]. I was overjoyed that the audience was so spontaneous every time you left the stage. And I was amazed that the reviews didn't headline your work. But they didn't. Nobody recognizes Nijinsky when they see him.

About Arts Club: Rue Shaw says that you have to have

Cage's enthusiasm for the young dancer is clear. Martha Graham and Dance Company, of which Cunningham was now a member, had performed at Chicago's Civic Opera House the week before in a program that included the premiere of Graham's *Land Be Bright*, with music by Arthur Kreutz and sets and costumes by Charlotte Trowbridge. Cunningham performed the role of the Yankee Orator, Erick Hawkins the role of the fictional Indian Chingachgook (from James Fenimore Cooper's *Leatherstocking Tales*), and Graham herself the role of Betsy Ross. From the start Cage is a champion of Cunningham's talent, something we'll see for decades to come. Cage briefly references "Jean," meaning Jean Erdman, another member of the Graham Company who was married to the mythologist Joseph Campbell, with whom Cunningham often was paired, and with whom he

concerts someplace else before she can give one at the Club. She is crazy about your work and felt rotten saying that, but that's what the conclusion was. Please don't be discouraged. I told her that you felt the same way about New York, that you wanted to do someplace else first. Bennington should be that possibility. Plus perhaps (I don't know anything about it) Yale Theatre, someplace in colleges: Cornell, Harvard. Rue also said: I wish when Merce starts with Jean that their music is not piano music because everybody no longer likes typical dance concert music. One more piano is only doubling the error. It was better when Louis had snare, wind and percussion and dance deal. What do you think? Giving it later in NY. Of course my fear is that people are anxious to say that our music is not enough by itself and must have dance, but I would not feel that way with you and Jean. At any rate work hard and we'll see you in June. If the radio thing goes through here, I'll let you know when and if possible maybe you'll play in it.

Yours and to Jean and Joe,
John

---

was preparing programs that would showcase their own choreography. They would give their first program togeth-er with fellow dancer Nina Fonaroff at Bennington College on August 1, 1942, a program they reprised in New York City later that year, on October 20 and 21, at the Humphrey-Weidman Studio Theatre, with an important addition: *Totem Ancestor* (1942), a solo work by Cunningham with new music by John Cage. *Totem Ancestor* is still one of very few works by Cunningham to be recorded in Labanotation (by Lena Belloc).

[Undated, postmarked June 20, 1942]
323 East Cermak Road, Chicago

Dear Merce:

Coming to NY next week around the 25th.
Please see Jean and letter to her. and Joe.
CBS in NY only got bad d[e]rogatory letters.
Where is Joyce.
Where will we get job.
Will be poor.

[Xenia's portion, handwritten:]
It's not as awful as J. says.
Except we are scared a little.
Have to build a little nest somewhere.

        Yrs —

        X.

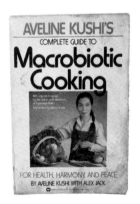

Cage's comment that the broadcast of *The City Wears a Slouch Hat* solicited only "d[e]rogatory" letters isn't entirely true, as the responses received by the radio stations in both New York and Chicago were in actuality quite mixed. Cage's mother, Lucretia ("Crete"), was one of the letter writers, then residing with Cage's father, the inventor, John Milton Cage, Sr., in Montclair, New Jersey. She was proud as a peacock, especially after having received a laudatory letter herself from an acquaintance, one Ruth Lord Jenkins, who found the "ocean surge" at the end of the work the "apotheosis of interpretive music." The broadcast even solicited a long and extremely thoughtful letter from a young composer who would in time garner his own following, the 25-year-old Robert Erickson.

Dear Merce:

      Coming to NY next week around the 25th.

      Please see Jean and letter to her. and Joe.

      CBS in NY only got bad drogatory letters:

      Where is Joyce.

      Where will we get job.

      Will be poor.

It's not as awful as J. says.
Except we are scared a little.
Have to build a little nest somewhere.
              yrs -
                X.

[Undated, postmarked June 28, 1943]
[New York]

Dear Merce:

Saturday night nearly went crazy, because, not solving my problems until they occur, I very suddenly realized you were gone. Fly away with you but was in a zoo.

Sunday, interested? Woke up in time to see you, worried whether you had taxi fund, etc. but was helpless; went through hottest day of y[ea]r in and out of bath tub. A parade went under the window (a real one) with something like 5 percussion bands, one of them made of black people played beautifully; it must have been a chinoiserie about your having gone away.

I don't know when it was that I found out how to let this month go by without continual sentimental pain. It's very simple now, because I'm looking forward to seeing you again rather than backward to having seen you recently. That's a happy way to be.

Another thing: I'm going to look at studios for you, not that I'm doing something you probably want to do yourself, but it

---

Cunningham earned very little money, so Cage invited him to work with him on projects he was doing for his father, who often took on war-effort projects for the government. At the time, this seems mostly to have involved translating medical articles by Spanish physicians, which is curious, since neither Cage nor Cunningham was ever known to be even remotely fluent in Spanish. This letter makes the first reference to their work together, but we see elaboration in Cage's letters postmarked July 2, 1943 and July 13, 1943. Cunningham was often touring and thus on the road— between 1942 and 1946 Cage sent letters to him in New York (c/o Martha Graham, 66 5th Avenue), at Bennington College in Bennington, Vermont, in both Provincetown and Boston, Massachusetts, in Steamboat Springs, Colorado, in Salt Lake City, Utah, in Washington, D.C., in Cincinnati, Ohio, in

will be good to give you a list, descriptions, etc., and then you'll know that such and such exists. I've gathered that you want to be uptown.

By Friday or so you should get new article to translate, which is long and will be very remunerative.

I say I'm unsentimental but I'm sitting at one of our tables and looking in a mirror where you often were.

We had a card this morning from the Patchens who are at Mt. Pleasant for the summer (!).

Please try writing to the Academy of M. care of the Library.

I don't know: this gravity elastic feeling to let go and fall together with you is one thing, but it is better to live exactly where you are with as many permanent emotions in you as you can muster. Talking to myself.

Your spirit is with me. Did you send it or do I just have it?

Yrs.
John

Oakland, California, and, finally, in Centralia, Washington, this last Cunningham's place of birth and where he was visiting his parents. Cage instructs him to write back to him in care of the Academy of Music Library, a movie theater named for the opera house that had once been situated across the street at E. 14th St. and Irving Place (which was apparently amenable to serving as Cage's post office, at least for a spell). The Cages by this time had moved to New York City, still very much married, and the blossoming relationship between the two men was initially clandestine.

[Undated, postmarked June 29, 1943]
[No location indicated]

Rain finally came + it's beautifully cool. Wonder how long it will last. It was marvelous because it started suddenly and then was alternately terrific and gentle.

I think of you all the time and therefor have little to say that would not embarrass you, for instance my first feeling about the rain was that it was like you.

Yesterday, with no success, I looked for a studio for you, found one that was useless for $125.00.

Otherwise the day was spent packing instruments, and studying the corporate structure of non-profit organizations, so that the Natl. Inst. for Biochem-Research would get under way legally. God knows why they didn't employ a lawyer.

This morning rode elegant us-bus to Academy. Thought about enigma and his little friend.

Someday maybe instead of writing I'll send you a present.

I hope you're having a beautiful time. Love you.

This letter signals the start of a more intimate relationship. "Enigma and his little friend" is Cage's playful reference to his and Cunningham's penises. "Enigma" refers to Cunningham's, while "his little friend" refers to Cage's own.

[Undated, postmarked July 2, 1943]
550 Hudson St., New York

Prince,

Very exciting to get your spirit letter no questions asked (we have a post office). I am this day sending long forty to 50 dollar article which I hope won't be travail to translate. At least you will get to know 3 more of your South American brothers.

When they (Benn[ington] Folk) get too intellectual, "answer them only with" art. Horror news: W. Lathrop has been subsidized by private individ. to go look at S.W. Indians and then when return to N.Y. occurs will be subsid. to nauseate us via theatre. Saw him in proper place: subway.

The weather here now is magical. Cool and sunny, it's like San Francisco.

I get terribly lonesome for you. Had a note from Renata who is in Colorado looking at MTS; she wants to see more of us and play percussion.

Sent my score to be published actually never thought that

The Martha Graham Company was in residence at Bennington College throughout much of 1943, hence Cage gives Cunningham a bit of advice as to how to deal with academics (note the nod to e.e. cummings in Cage's remark "answer them only with," which appears in cummings' "O sweet spontaneous," first published in 1920. Cage set cummings' poetry to music in his *Five Songs for Contralto* in 1938 and in his *Forever and Sunsmell* in 1942; in 1948, he would set one of the sonnets from cummings' *Unrealities of Tulips and Chimneys* in his own *Experiences II*). Also note Cage's catty "Horror news" remark, which references Welland Lathrop, an American dancer and choreographer who from 1930 to 1934 was resident at the Cornish School. Lastly, Cage's remark that "Every now + then the past smiles at me" refers to his own prepared piano, developed while he himself was

would occur. Made added note in it to arouse creative spirit in this land: "Determine size and position of mutes by experiment." Read an article about "Sordino" in a musical dict., which came to conclusion that a plain penny put between violin strings is better than fancy mute. Every now + then the past smiles at me.

Today I have to trace graphs about the male hormone.

I stop doing that every now and then + read your letter over again.

Please don't let intellectual art discussions intimidate you. They are only talking about art or loving it or God knows what, but you are it. You're a visitation and any one who has a chance to be near you is damned fortunate.

It's like the stories of people talking about God or Christ + he is Incognito among them.

I nearly left this earth a few minutes ago—ecstasy—word from you. Pretty soon I'll write music for you.

Love,

John

---

at Cornish. He first made use of it in his *Bacchanale* (1940), which accompanied a dance by a graduating student at the Cornish School, Syvilla Fort, who wanted a score with an African "inflection." As the story goes, Cage had intended to write for percussion ensemble. However, because the performance space was small and he had only a grand piano with which to work, he began experimenting with objects placed inside the instrument—under and between its strings—in an effort to alter its sounds. The rest, as they say, is history. Cage's magnum opus for the instrument, *Sonatas & Interludes* (1946–1948), would in time receive citations from both the Guggenheim Foundation and the National Academy of Arts and Letters for having "extended the boundaries of music."

[Undated, postmarked July 2, 1943]
550 Hudson St., New York

Dear

Thank you for sending translation so promptly; words not known are few + familiar to me because of my "extensive med. readings," i.e. xeroftalmia = xerophthalmia. I am a little confused about luetic, lues, etc., which I find means syphilis in some dicts. + just the pox in others.

Library doesn't seem to have any real Sp. Med. Dict. I am at wit's end because we are going to go to Roocky Rook with Watts + I have to pick up shoes for Mother + 1000 other things. Translation is marvelous and Dr. Freyre is not only hamstrung but a fool verbally.

Needed you 1,0000,000 x as much as ever this morning. Have to beat it (if I can procure a Sp. Med. Dict. will send it to you).

Love, J.

Much of this letter would be unfathomable had we not earlier learned that Cage and Cunningham were working together translating Spanish medical articles for Cage's father. "Xeroftalmia = xerophthalmia"? "Luetic, lues, etc."?? For his efforts in translating not quite 2,000 words, Cunningham was paid a whopping $14.80.

[along the left margin:]
Discovery: no Sp. Med. Dict. exists!!!

[second page:]
after counting words in article, find there are not quite 2,000; will send money order for $14.80.

I am on open top bus writing.

Writing and dying.

Yr. joint letter beautiful.

Pull a pig tail for me.

Need you to lie next to me under, on top, inside, between, close, close.

[Undated, postmarked July 7, 1943]
550 Hudson St., New York

Lover:

Now in dark of 2nd week; look like battled and scarred person (mostly from fatal weekend in N.J., country not seeming to agree with me unless you are there): a boil, 50,000,000 bites and blisters, general debility.

Two letters from you (one at home + one at library), and I, glad that the translation business interests you: will send new article presently.

This morning all the parts of me that haven't heard that you are away got me up and out early and longing to lie down beside you.

Country had a special moment when your spirit reached me in leafy place and mad embrace. Would love to share with you if even pigtail. The trivia people may have tangents that you will luminesce if you get close enough, like dead (otherwise) tubes brought into electric atmosphere.

Erotic references in this letter abound! Cage's use of the word *oestrus* in its last line is perhaps telling, being the medical term (in its Latin spelling) that denotes the recurring period of sexual receptivity and fertility in many female mammals, excluding humans, more commonly referred to as being "in heat." Cage even manages to sexualize one of his father's many patents: his "Mist-A-Cold," which related "generally to aspiratory devices and more particularly to an improved inhaler, suitable for oral or nasal inhalation" (patent no. 2,579,362). "Thought you'd be amused to know," says Cage to Cunningham, "that Dad's newest inhalation medicine is designed to increase the male's resistance to orgasm."

Loves:

How in dark of 2nd
week; looks like battled
and scarred person (mostly
from fatal week end
in N.J., country not
seeming to agree with
me unless you are
there); a boil, 50,000,000
bites and blisters, general
debility.

Two letters from you
(one at home + one
at library), and I,

glad that the translation business interests you: Will send new article presently.

This morning, all the parts of me that haven't heard that you are away got me up and on early and longing to lie down beside you.

Country has a special
moment when your
spirit reached me
in leafy place
and mad embrace
Would love to
share with you
if even pigtail
The trivia people
may have tangents
that will luminesce
if you get close
enough, like dead
(otherwise) tubes

brought into electric
atmosphere.
I love the peace and
beauty and absence of
elegance connoisseurs.
Your words paint
ight land.

Love you,

Starved for good long
fuck with you.

Postscripts

Thought you'd be
amused to know
that Dad's newest
inhalation medicine
~~is designed to increase~~
the male's resistance
~~to orgasm.~~

Maybe you're angry
or disgusted because
I write too full of
desire and getting
sexy.

They are taking down
the Enemy display.
Passing by, saw "S THIS
FOR YOU".

Make me a dance
that is a sex-love
dance, sans frustration.

I am in oestrus
now thinking of
you — such a
full-fledged need.

I love the peace and beauty and absence of elegance connoisseurs. Your words paint idyll land.

Love you,
J.

Starved for good long fuck with you.

Postscripts:

Thought you'd be amused to know that Dad's newest inhalation medicine is designed to increase the male's resistance to orgasm.

Maybe you're angry or disgusted because I write too full of desire and getting sexy.

They are taking down the Enemy display. Passing by, saw 'S THIS FOR YOU.'

Make me a dance that is a sex love dance, sans frustration.

I am in oestrus now thinking of you—such a full-fledged need.

[Undated, postmarked July 9, 1943]
550 Hudson St., New York

Prince:

They've lost the magazine I need to have photostatted for you.
That is why I haven't sent new article yet. They will either find it
or I will locate in other library other copy.

I am gradually recovering from diseases and am dimly aware
that ½ of time is practically past. The idea of seeing you in a little
more than 2 weeks is marvelous and exciting and I have to stop
thinking about it. I'm writing on the bus + have to get off and mail
this. You invent love fraises of you and say them from me to you.

J.

This mundane little letter has a sweet play on words at its
close: *fraises* in lieu of phrases, in French, strawberries.

[Undated, postmarked July 13, 1943]
550 Hudson St., New York

I am depressed and lonesome, pay no attention if I go to miasma. Outer world seems odious. Spirit must be out of me, off in some leafy place with yours. Fortunately, job of making illiterate translation literate is long, doing it is like being with you and is what I need. A letter late yesterday from you, love you. (Library found magazine: had consigned it to basement; photostats are being rushed and you will get them this week (a shorter article with pictures, to which pay no spatial intention, but please do translate notes for pictures).)

Joyce is coming! A new level of consciousness for NY. Bunny thinks she will be here middle of next week.

She will write to you because we told her [about] Bennington. We are all sitting in pools of inner and outer humidity now: weather is abominable. Although I wish you back as soon as you can come, unless you need to for other reason be body-free to wander. This is too horrible a place when not absolutely necessary.

The "Joyce" that is coming is Joyce Wike, an anthropology student at the University of Washington who took dance classes at the Cornish School. She was one of Cunningham's most colorful friends, and it has been posited that her interest in the legends and ceremonial practices of the aboriginal inhabitants of the region inspired his interest in the Pacific Northwest Indian "spirit dance," a solo form. Wike was reputedly an excellent ballroom dancer, and she and Cunningham were known to go out dancing in the evening and not return until the wee hours of the morning. And it would be through Wike that Cage and Cunningham would come to know the artist Mark Tobey, with Morris Graves one of two Pacific Northwest artists whose work they would come to champion. The one and only time I met Joyce Wike, years later, was in the lobby of a theater in Seattle during the

Arrived at Library too early so am now sitting in arboreal sunken garden, making thoughts about you.

You must help me to come to some definite point of view about whether you like or can stand this dull research kind of work. If what I have been planning happens, you would have a job, but it would not be translating much of the time, but it would be dull and I don't want to drive you insane, but purpose was concerned with money and way for you to have it. It seems a solution when money is thought of. But last week I had to distinguish for endless hours between androsterone, androstanedione, androstenedione, androstenediol, androstanediol, methyl-3-keto-androstanol, etc. etc. 'til maddened. Only variety was in testosterone, methyl testosterone + testosterone benzoate. And now this week again same words.

I think the answer for you is to have this to do when not remunerated otherwise. If you see the Muse, send her to me, if she remembers me at all. Had dismal time trying to get in musical touch; contact is lost. Am at dangerous point where I imagine that inspiration will ultimately come if I just don't do anything about

intermission of a program given by the Merce Cunningham Dance Company. After learning who I was, she loudly berated herself for not having worn the colorful patchwork vest that Xenia had long ago made for her that still hung in her bedroom closet.

it. But actually working is being avoided and that is what I must stop doing.

Nor have I been conscientious about studio hunting: problem is too great for me.

———————————————

Today is truly bleak day for me. You cannot write to Library any longer: they object. Sorry this letter is so miserable.

I can't get any letters from you anymore but will go on reading ones I already have and pretty soon see you.

I really feel happier than this letter is, which was written this morning; but it contains some information of some value.

Check will come but tardily because it will have to go on new expense acct. Will be for $40.00.

Saturday *[postmarked July 17, 1943]*
550 Hudson St., New York

Prince:

Here is remuneration and compressed volumes of desire to see
you. Some kind of mad control is being in me that I don't go crazy
stark because I need you.

   We don't know when Joyce will arrive if she should it would
be added stimulus to come see pas d'action; however have doubts,
malheureusement.

   Activities are beginning to show: Bunny will be busy now +
for some time on screens which have been constructed + are to be
picked up today.

   Lou is thinking about a new mag. for young composers to
rant in.

   Those Argentine doctors were idiots but we will probably
never know them too well.

   Am anxious to know how you feel about Martha creation +
whether she has given you more than cartwheels to do.

By all accounts, Cage and Xenia were an amiable and
affectionate couple. This letter references Cage's nickname
for his wife, "Bunny," which was also Xenia's nickname for
her husband. Decades later, long after their divorce, Cage
would occasionally telephone her, just to say hello. When he
learned she was unhappy living in New York as she aged,
he offered to provide her with the funds necessary to take
a trip out west to see if there might be a better place to live.
She was deeply offended and hung up. Cage's remark about
Graham ("Martha") giving Cunningham "more than cartwheels to do," by the way, is the first intimation we see of
what will become Cage's insistence that Cunningham strike
out on his own.

I may have surprise for you when you get back.

Has anything happened about your Rodeo connections?

Need you, love you.

Letter came this morning: going to sea and sun will be marvelous, but please be lonesome enough to come back in not too distant time; I couldn't help thinking how magic it would be to meet you some place on cliff or sand, but problems of communication and my own allergy to summer-nature mock romanticism.

No new word from Indian.

Martha's dance sounds like maybe beauty. I hope it remains in intimacy; if it is tortured there, I can worship; but if it gets to "heights of frustration greatness," would have difficulty.

I've found out that my muse's name is Euterpe. This does not incline me farther in direction of the art.

I hope I'm right in thinking you rec'd. 2nd money order for long article. No mention in letter. I have new translation and will send check for it next Friday or Saturday. If you want money mailed to sea-shore place, let me know. ($13.25)

Rudy Reviel has arranged a meeting for me with man who runs Blue Angel. La Touche is back from Congo and persuaded

There are various references in these early letters to Cage's "allergy" to sun and nature. By 1954, this must have at least abated, since being, as he said, "starved for nature," he moved for a time to the Gate Hill Cooperative, a.k.a. "The Land," in Stony Point, New York. There he rediscovered not only his great love of the outdoors but an enthusiasm for mushrooms that would last a lifetime. And despite the aversions, he expresses to Cunningham in a later letter his desire to vacation with him "in nature." Note also here that Cage's dissatisfaction with Euterpe (in Greek mythology the muse of music) prompted his later adoption of Calliope (the muse presiding over eloquence and epic poetry, according to Ovid the "chief of all muses"). Cunningham's muse was, of course,

B.A. that I should be attraction there. At first thought it would be all right, but since have changed my mind: I am so completely on fringe of acceptability that such an action would remove what of doubt remains in bourgeois heads. Cannot discuss this with Euterpe since we do not get on together; would prefer to discuss it with you.

I love you and often think of fancy reasons why: spirit is very close to me and mine, I sent it, close to you.

Have Buenos tiempos y coloratura benefices y comprobar natura.

Translation was much better this time and easier to get into shape.

There is one more to be done, but no time to get Photostats, etc., before you leave (besides you're probably sick of Spanish medical language).

My whole desire is to run up and down the sea coast looking for you.

Love

_____

Terpsichore, her name deriving from the Greek words for "delight" and "dance." Lastly, The Blue Angel, among New York City's early supper clubs, which officially opened its doors at 152 E. 55th St. on April 14, 1943.

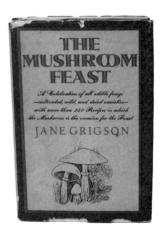

[Undated, postmarked August 17, 1943]
[No location indicated]

Reason not having written: misinterpreted word soon wanted duration to lack.

Am so near insanity you speak of (am in it) that begin to hate (not you) self.

Today shaking from yesterday's bottle.

I do not want you to come back if this letter is the reason for return (that too is why I haven't written because entreaty is all to you in my hands (and what pleasure is there in a gift that's begged?)). So please be deaf and blind and only know I always love you.

God! With what impatience I expect your coming, and how will it take place? Where you and I, and the details, moving pictures which disfeature everything else in my mind.

I swear you're with me constantly (please do not feel

Cage admits he is "shaking from yesterday's bottle," not his first reference in the present collection to his having had too much to drink. He and Xenia were notorious party people, and over-imbibing was reputedly one of their favorite social activities. By the time he reached his mid-70s, Cage had long before stopped smoking, but his drinking was still in excess. (At night, he would draw a line halfway down the wine bottle with a marking pen so that he would know when to stop. In the morning, I'd inevitably find the level of wine in the bottle well below it.) His doctors suggested that alcohol (and particularly wine) was likely the cause of his recurring eczema, and recommendation was made that he drink only single-malt liquors instead, far less complicated for the system. He did, at first with some enthusiasm, but a year or so before his death he stopped drinking altogether. (Although,

Reason not having written : misinter
preted word soon wanted duration
to lack

am so near insanity you
speak of (am in it) that
begin to hate (not you) self.
Today shaking from yesterday's
bottle.

I do not want you to come
back if this letter is the
reason for return (that too
is why I haven't written
because entreaty is all to you
in my hands (and what
pleasure is there in a
gift that's begged?)) so
please be deaf and blind

and only know I always
love you

God! with what impatience
I expect your coming, and
how will it take place?
where you and I and the
details, moving pictures,
which disfeature everything
else in my mind

I swear you're with me
constantly (please do not
feel responsible or pulled
away from center, which
I know for you is myster
and beneficially not for
you in me or other).

kiss

responsible or pulled away from center, which I know for you is mystery and beneficially not for you in me or other).

Kiss

---

on December 31, 1991, which would be Cage's last New Year's Eve, after pouring generous glasses of champagne for me and Merce just before the stroke of midnight, he poured an inch for himself, gulped it down, washed his glass, and that was that.)

Fat letter from Social Security Board here. Shall I forward it? All things happening not of too good a nature: Bunny hurt her foot (but it's getting better); Robin apartment rented by others; Jean Erdm. wants to give a concert with me and over phone sounded good because it was to be made from beginning + travel through rasas, etc. But find it is to include all former works and would not be of a piece which was what interested me over phone. Told her so. Would like to begin with creative and continue the journey. Musical interludes of Harrison and Yrs. truly. Lou's friend, Sherm, was about to surprise Lou, dropping in from California, but, horribly drowned off coast of N.J. without ever seeing him. Lou is ready to jump off a bridge. Only good thing now is Bunny's new mobile which is magnificent and everybody can tell it seeing it. The screens were photographed by [a] Japanese man who said they could be in temples in India, China, or even some places in Japan. Nothing pleases me more than the Orient springing up in our midst.

Xenia was the daughter of the Archpriest of the Eastern Orthodox Russian-Greek Church of Alaska, the Reverend Andrew Petrovich Kashevaroff, and Marfa E. ("Marta") Kashevaroff (née Bolshanin). Xenia was a former art student at Reed College in Oregon and in time would leave her own mark as a sculptor of abstract mobiles, a bookbinder, and a conservator. She was small and feisty, childhood polio causing her to walk with a slight limp, and she possessed what Cage called a "barb wit." (It would be the tubercular destruction of Xenia's left knee that would in late 1943/early 1944 exempt her "sole-breadwinner" husband from the draft.) Cunningham much later recounted a dance program they'd attended together in New York City. Cunningham enjoyed the soloist's performance, but Xenia was nonplussed. "Don't you think she's improved?" he asked. Xenia wryly replied,

Read in paper that you will not go to New Haven.

It's very peaceful to come here where [there] are so many signs of spirit I love. You left everything in such spotless state.

I feel very quiet and very calm and I think it's because that's the way we were last together.

Love you

"That's the problem." This letter also contains one of two references in the present collection to Xenia's "screens," and one can only assume she'd turned her artistic attention to room dividers. (Interestingly, there is a particularly con-founding story in Cage's later *Indeterminacy: New Aspect of Form in Instrumental and Electronic Music* involving screens, a Japanese abbot, and Hollywood, which might well harken back to this aspect of Xenia's work.) Lastly, Cage's note about the shocking death of Lou Harrison's friend "Sherm" is referencing Sherman Slayback, a salesman (later jukebox repairman) with whom Harrison had a relationship shortly after graduating from high school. Slayback had gone swim-ming off the New Jersey shoreline with his brother-in-law, John Manfred Larson, and both men drowned (September 14, 1943).

Just love and to say wish you success at 1st appearance. Hope you have fun along this path.

Forwarding letter from your father and one from Zellmer; do you want the Social Security one?

The tiny and the big worlds; I know little about either.

Always yours

[Undated, postmarked September 25, 1943]
[No location indicated]

Thank you for beauty letter. Please don't worry about horror-clichés etc. of show business and being bored: perhaps stand for it. Almost for everyone is some kind of horror in life and it is best if it is outside of one as in this case. In it you must be fully beautiful and be exception but brilliantly and not with disgust. Remaining time and activity will be stronger for it: e.g., Rousseau, Charles Ives, etc., etc. and Rilke's written a Letter about it.

I have looked quickly over dance play (because I have to get back rapidly—will read more again) and it is not written in order enough for me to have reading from which to criticize. The words in it are continually alive. Now and then the rhythm stumbles or gets in phraseology too consciously archaic. When you get back, suggest you put it all in order. I do not yet feel all characters are well-presented (in other words, idea and plot are still in your mind and not yet given as blood to characters; this time in particular felt girl to be undrawn). However it is better-bodied than last time

---

Cage's reference to "dance play" here is to his *Four Walls*, for which Cunningham was laboriously writing a libretto. We see in Cage's short list of things he's forwarding to Cunningham a letter from Pvt. John C. Cunningham, the youngest of the three Cunningham boys, known familiarly as "Jack," who was at the time serving in the U.S. Army. Interesting to note that Jack died exactly two weeks after his brother Merce. Their older brother, Dorwin, after serving for years as a judge in Lewis County Superior Court in Washington, died in 2004.

read and see no earthly reason for scrapping. Will say more next letter.

Forwarding 3 things: from   Georgia

Pvt. John C. Cunningham

Social S.

Love.

Your stove came, is dark
and beautiful.

Whole place is dark because
it's night now and I'm
lonesome for you.

Writing music with more
impetus.

Bunny's making many new
mobiles, and screens installed
tomorrow and many more
new publicity things, etc.

Great surprise which you
will see.

I'm sorry your heart was
sick — maybe well now

When will you be back
What kind of land will
we be together in?

Need you.

[Undated, postmarked September 28, 1943]
[No location indicated]

Your stove came, is dark and beautiful.

Whole place is dark because it's night now and I'm lonesome for you.

Writing music with more impetus.

Bunny's making many new mobiles, and screens installed tomorrow and many more new publicity things, etc.

Great surprise which you will see.

I'm sorry your heart was sick—maybe well now.

When will you be back?

What kind of land will we be together in?

     Need you.

[This note, contained in a very small envelope, without postmark, is fragile and has been cut up into small pieces, some of which, folded, have over time broken in two. The fragments, comprising everything extant, have been pieced together.]

i am in a world you make with recherches: and the leaf is suspended by a pin near the little wooden saint. these things mean very much to me; but i think it is not to my credit that they do. i am beginning to think that the reason i "give so much" is that i am so poor in spirit, hoping through leaning on every little gesture, thought, word, and mood of other to get my empty spaces filled. so my giving is really demanding. where shall i go and what shall i do: read a book? how to benefit by what can be said by oneself!

not being spontaneous and relaxed about natural things, i get ideas about people connected with art, fashion little pedestals,

While undated, this letter is synchronous with Xenia's decision to leave her husband, moving in late February 1944 out of their shared Hudson St. apartment and back, if briefly, to Peggy Guggenheim's mansion on Beekman Place where she and Cage had first stayed upon their arrival in New York. She never looked back, and the two would divorce in 1945. (Xenia appeared alone as the plaintiff in a district court in Idaho, Cage agreeing in advance to her complaint by formal stipulation. He was ordered to pay $100 per month in alimony, which he did to his dying day.) From all accounts, Xenia was permissive about sex, her own youthful amorous adventures an entirely open secret. (While in high school she was known to have been sexually involved with Ed Ricketts, a marine biologist and pioneer ecologist living in California's Carmel Valley, and the photographer Edward

love them and bring the public in. a rather disgusting scene.

i love you always.

xenia went all alone.

beauty.

i am in a muddled state.

calliope calls.

soul-searching; i did it once before, about 12 years ago. i'm not very good at it.

louis and satie at breakfast, what did that mean?

Weston, another of her erstwhile lovers, once described her as "most delightfully unmoral, pagan.") At the time of their meeting, Cage was involved with a man, Don Sample (with whom he'd traveled companionably throughout Europe after aborted college studies and then cohabitated with for a time after returning to Los Angeles), and at the time of their engagement, with another woman, Pauline Schindler (41 years old to Cage's 22, the estranged wife of the famous architect, Rudolph Schindler), who was living in the bucolic Ojai Valley. But something about her husband's affair with Cunningham had become for her irreconcilable.

[Undated, postmarked July 3, 1944]
[No location indicated]

your letters i just plain love: they bring you so close that at any moment i expect the door will open and you will see me camouflaged in enigmatic home, built on shoes you made.

i went away for week-end; but you will be disappointed to know it was to Buchanan's in New Jersey plus Virgil [Thomson]. However, it was quite pleasant, and everything was taken easily. There were not many bugs; it was cool; there were two yelling children, but on the whole well-behaved, and Virgil was in kind style. Drinks, swimming, damn good food; but best of all was the music and talks about music. Virgil had brought out one of the rare copies of Satie's *Socrate*, and we must have played and sung it six times. I know now many things wrong with *Four Walls* musically, basic of all being that i made too much expressiveness via melody-means. Some time i [will] make better music for you. *Socrate* is an incredibly beautiful work. There is no expression in the music or in the words, and the result is that it is

Cage's devotion to the French composer Erik Satie, captured so beautifully here in his account of a weekend spent in the country with the American composer and music critic Virgil Thomson, would express itself variously throughout Cage's life. Cage and Thomson first met at Mills College, becoming fast friends, and Thomson wrote enthusiastically about Cage's early works in the *New York Herald Tribune*, where he was chief music critic. (The two would later fall out over Cage's contribution to *Virgil Thomson: His Life and Music* [published in 1959], a book commissioned by Thomson in which Cage opined that Thomson's music would not survive the test of time.) "Buchanan's" is the country home in Denville, New Jersey, of Briggs W. Buchanan, who was the object of Thomson's amorous attentions while the two men were students at Harvard University. This love was

68

overpoweringly expressive. The melody is simply an atmosphere which floats. The accompaniment is a continuous juxtaposition of square simplicities. But the combination is of such grace! Three pieces: the first is after a banquet, and Socrates is merely introduced by a little speech which rather completely avoids any profundity. The second piece is in the country, and Socrates and his companion talk about the history of the spot and how delightful the air and grass is, and there is a slight suggestion that following the conversation they lie down together on the grass. The third piece is a report of the death of Socrates, little things he said, little things the jailer said, how it was when he drank the poison and only at the very end is it finally said that he was "the most just, etc. great of men." Sometimes I played it while Virgil tortured the air with song; mostly, however, he preferred to both play and sing, while I turned pages. We also went thru *Four Saints*, *Filling Station*, a piano sonata, a good deal of Mozart; and one evening *The Perilous Night*. Virgil went into ecstasy which will not get into print. I am genius, and everything i write is fine he says and he says related to great things, etc. I cannot remember it all.

---

unrequited, however, and two years after graduation from college, Buchanan met and married Florence Reynaud, with whom he fathered two sons (Briggs, Jr., and David George). In time, Thomson found himself integrated into a very normal heterosexual family and he occasionally used the Buchanan's home as a genial meeting place to entertain his friends.

Cage would soon undertake an arrangement for solo piano of the first movement of Satie's *Socrate*, to which Cunningham contributed a choreographic aspect, *Idyllic Song*. This collaboration was presented as part of their first out-of-town program in Richmond, Virginia, on November 18, 1944. Cage also again references *Four Walls* (1944) for solo piano and voice, used as music for the eponymous dance play by Cunningham which would be first performed in Steamboat

Who cares?

Country was beautiful, and lying on the grass so that i could sometimes see the net a tree is against the sky or turning make a space for eyes between two trees and watch bird-movements across and in it. Beautiful daisies and a jungle of tiger lilies. Multitudinous lakes and canoes. I could tell how distinctly happy you would be in country wherever; and i really need not be with you for me or for you, because there was facility in inventing your presence and knowing that just then you were merely not visible or not audible.

Springs, Colorado, on August 22, 1944. Cunningham's text, also referenced variously herein, was titled "Sweet love my throat is gurgling." Cunningham's dance is programmatic, its theme one of a dysfunctional family, while Cage's music is entirely diatonic. And note mention of *The Perilous Night* (1943–44) for solo prepared piano, another dramatic work that reflects Cage's emotional turmoil at the time. Perhaps significantly, this is one of very few of Cage's early pieces that would *not* be paired with a dance by Cunningham.

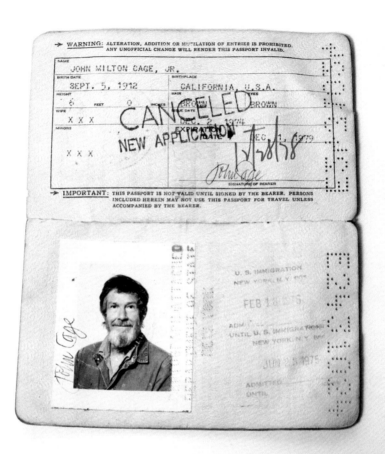

J. Cage
12 E. 17Th St.
NYC 3

Merce Cunningham
c/o Perry Mansfield School
Steamboat Springs,
Colorado.

please kiss whatever part of you you can reach for me.

i found a marvelous shark's jaw.

and dreams

[Undated, postmarked July 12, 1944]
12 E. 17th St., New York

au prince delicieux.

your last letter is so beautiful i cannot answer it, only read it and lie on it.

music going beautifully, peace and fluently; i will hear it again tomorrow but this time with fizdale because he senses phrase which gearhart does not know.

saw king's row which is very fine. went to amagansett and ny coktail group. swam in ocean and now have night-itchy sunburn. bicycled all over small hills.

i have two movements finished: seven to go; i think i have not written so well before. heard berg's violin concerto reading score as record played at lou's. it is very beautiful except when it gets chewingummy re intervals (da da da de; da da da do).

Did you meet the Cages in Denver?

bell sounds will enter now with crossing of the hands; utter grace is the goal.

This letter is short and sweet, albeit hinting at Cage's increasingly disquieted state. New York summers were warm, and Cage spent a lot of time in air-conditioned movie theaters. (Decades later, living with Cunningham in New York in their 18th St. loft, also without air conditioning, Cage would cope with hot and humid days by drinking copious amounts of McGrath's Irish Tea on ice.) He's recently seen *Kings Row* (1942), he reports, directed by Sam Wood and starring Ann Sheridan, Robert Cummings, and Ronald Reagan. This was Reagan's most notable role during his early acting career at Warner Brothers. When queried some 40 years later, during Reagan's presidency, whether he was in support of the president, Cage thought for a moment and then replied, "Well, if we have to have an actor for president, I'd prefer a good one—like Greta Garbo."

the heat is not too bad and besides I live in the nude;
do beauty work (another secret: inexpressivity)
i am often in deep pain; i am afraid i am not human being
i talk to you all day long but when i start to write i cannot

it would be madness this summer were i not working and in
casa enigma. thank god the muse is good to me. otherwise
pain of not being near you would carry me off. AU PRINCE
DES MONTAGNES: L'AIR EST SI FRAIS ET SI DELICIEUX.

[Undated, postmarked July 13, 1944]
12 E. 17th St., New York

would be god-like to be in mountain country with you but am chained to city rock making music-fire. am having muse-luck, but like you beserk from lack of sex-love—letters are my bed and dream-stimulating. would fly by night if could lie in your arms and explode against a tautness. need you

just finished copying music so far written and will hear it tonight. had insane lunch with Schuyler. he wants me to write jazz for billy rose! he didn't like music for 4 walls; and, by the way if it sounds bad or makes trouble personally or artistically, throw it away. no feelings from here because it was pleasure to write, but could have done better under other time-circumstances.

i close my eyes so that you can come through the door. i wonder how it will be when i see you next: at the station, or here, or in the woods or ocean, or a cocktail at the ritz; please, can it be near ocean? or in the night with no words.

glad theatre is good and large. i begin to sing for new song.

Cunningham was engaged for six weeks in the summer of 1944 to teach at the Perry-Mansfield Workshop, a summer arts camp run by Charlotte Perry and Portia Mansfield in Steamboat Springs, Colorado, on the slopes of the Rocky Mountains. Hence Cage's moniker for Cunningham— PRINCE DES MONTANES—at the letter's close. The Cage-Cunningham collaborative work *Four Walls* would have its premiere in Steamboat Springs later that summer, complete with Cunningham's text and performed by a cast of sixteen dancers, including Cunningham. In early 1945, Cunningham would excerpt his solo from *Four Walls* for a new work titled *Soliloquy.*

it would be madness this summer were i not working and in casa enigma. thank god the muse is good to me. otherwise pain of not being near you would carry me off. AU PRINCE DES MONTANES: L'AIR EST SI FRAIS ET SI DELICIEUX.

John

Today is muse-day: and Calliope was good. Et Terpsichore?

Third movement is now finished, to be heard tomorrow. First two movements sound marvelously: Fizdale could play it and the whole thing went smoothly and as though it were right. I made a few changes on hearing both pianos do it; but nothing basic. I am beginning to get grasp of situation which is a pleasure, to say the least. If third movement sounds anything like it should it will be miraculous. It is short and a little bit like a vision and a little bit like a magic fixation, although it has much more variety than i generally give. god, how i wish you could hear it. All this talk about movements is just so much rubbish. What actually takes place so far is this: For a little less than two minutes, only one line is heard at a time (gracefully, they converse); the following 6½ minutes are what i call the second movement but in reality merely continue from first with a variety of voices heard, sometimes one, sometimes 4, sometimes 2 or 3, etc. Sustaining pedal goes down sometimes on one piano, creating atmosphere for other to move

---

This letter, like others that follow, reveals much about Cage's work on his (not-yet-titled) *A Book of Music* (1944) for two prepared pianos, which he labored over for months. It would receive its first performance on January 21, 1945, at the New School for Social Research in New York by Robert Fizdale and Arthur Gold. (Years later, from 1956 to 1961, Cage himself would teach at the New School, giving five sequential courses: "Experimental Composition," "Virgil Thomson: The Evolution of a Composer," "Erik Satie: The Evolution of a Composer," "Advanced Composition," and "Mushroom Identification.") Fizdale and Gold, who commissioned several important works for two pianos in the middle of the 20th century, were American duo pianists known cheerfully as "The Boys" in New York's artistic community. While

in; just before end of this part, everything rises and floats, and then settles into gentle single spot, which is sustained for two accelerating measures, so that third part is in new tempo (faster, and phrases changed accordingly so as to make the sections last equal length of time) with new sounds (not all new, but several of the sustained type); this lasts almost two minutes (like first part) and then you are where i am. And what i think now i will do is to have some louder sounds in chordal fashion with original tempo so that it is like a hymn for a wild church.

Cage would in time compose works for countless musicians, this was likely his first commission from professional performers.

[Undated, postmarked July 20, 1944]
12 E. 17th St., New York

Monsieur:

my muse fluidity continued and 4 movements are finished; last
night i was able to hear 3rd and 4th movements; i had thought
to copy 3rd movement yesterday, but I woke up so early that I
was here by seven and it was a beautiful day so i wrote the 4th
movement which got finished around two o'clock; and then i
had both pieces to copy so as to be able to hear them, did that,
had dinner, beginning to get jittery that they wouldn't "sound,"
bought some brandy and went to hear them. And thank God and
Calliope, they are marvelous. All four hold together like one big
movement and it is beautiful. The part i wrote to you about: the
faster part: is fantastic. It is like a scherzo in paradise. Instead
of writing hymn for wild church, I went back to original tempo
and really continued second movement in more passionate
vein. please hear it. i have been lucky and i am grateful. i had the
most curious experiences writing the 4th piece which came so
quickly: everything simply happened: phrases wrote themselves,
ignored, seemingly, my "phrase structure" and then turned out to
be on "phrase structure" side after all, making everything clear
but passionate. i drank too much brandy after i found out the
music was right, and i don't feel very good today, although i will
probably start next part. So far, piece is a little over 13 minutes.
That is approximately length of perilous night: except this music
holds together and is played without a break, but really it never
is boring because it is always having new things happening.
Have a new idea now upon which deliberation and dreaming
must center: to make next part prestissimo (out of my range of
execution) so that speed will enter for the spirit. i have never
really written any fast, really fast, music, and i think i will do it:

these unresonant sounds will take to it like water because they do not muddy each other. I am leaning towards the side of giving plain title like "Sonata for two pianos." That would involve me in tempo titles for movements: andante, etc., of which i would not be too pleased.... haven't heard from you for long week, except via spirit, which is what sustains me. will probably send little gift soon. the nights are no longer perilous, having moved into area of being terrifying. as darkness comes, i lose mind with loneliness and must work or go to movie to bring about utter fatigue which protects ... i hope you love it there and have some beauty one to love ... and i hope *Four Walls* is going well and that you are spirit-full ... what need to wish? ... you are strong ... love you

in one letter i said absurd things about
inexpressivity; obviously wrong, but what i
meant was that high expressivity often comes
about through no attempt to make it or to express
anything. had dinner one night with denby; i
think he's a sad little man who's frightened of
something. read his poetry which has some good
qualities, but is by no means off this earth.
i keep reading marvelous myths in joe's book,
but joe, too, is not really fine fine writer.
of course, this is first draft i have and he
will probably improve

letter i
would you like me to
send copy of
finnegan book which
is out now or would
you rather save that
for home-reading?

need you deliciously

gee bill came but
is nothing; do not
worry about it.

prestissimo will
be complex at
first, then simple
then complex and
then faster yet
to end entire piece
which should be
finished in two
weeks, because have
more things to write;
i am so happy with
this music that i
shall be sad when
it is all written
each sound has
gotten to be friendly
and something i know
and have pleasure
with; they are so
well trained, too.

send me some little
twig or a hair from
near enigma or a
piece of grass you
touched and sunbathed
with, mon prince.

today is beautiful and i am dreaming of you and enigma
and how we are together today: your words in my ears making
espirit soar and enigma beside and in me to make the body
glimp and taut by turns with delight. oh, i am sure we coul
use eachother today

                        i like to believe that you are writing
my music now: god knows i'm not doing it, because it simply
seems to happen the prestissimo is incredible the way you
are and is perhaps a description and song about you

                                                banalities;
blue check arrived and dv et helmsley got theirs; i am
afflicted with bills of all description, but do not seem to
be able to be sensible about money. passed by clyde's yesterday
and wanted to wrap it up and send it to you. what's wrong
with their socks; they look beautiful. had, for a change, a
pleasant time with schuyler; he informs me that oliver who
called the other day and wanted to know whether you could hold
a tune and what kind of voice you had, with robbins, has you
in mind for the lead of their dance-musical; it doesn't mean
you have to sing like galli-curci; but like american sailor
perhaps, instead: i really don't know anything but, can you
sing (and see stripes au meme temps?)

                                        there is apparently a
part in the book where you would go through a tunnel of love
and everyone thinks you would do it very well: so do i, please
go through mine, taking your time, if you will.

                                                also schuyler
had evening with virgil and v.t. now says i am ultra-genius,
having seen some of 2 piano work, and that i am on a par with
picasso, schoenberg, stravinsky, satie, matisse, cezanne,
van gogh, etc. ad nauseum: schuyler now thinks virgil had
good reasons for not reviewing other concerts, will blare
next one to skies, that his review of it is really already
written, that he has been making careful decisions about
what to say, etc. i don't like being great. it's not good
for my relation with calliope, who by the way, is not female,
and looks exactly like you.

                                pardon the intrusion: but when
in september will you be back? i would like to measure my
breath in relation to the air between us.

[Undated, postmarked July 22, 1944]
12 E. 17th St., New York

[This letter is intentionally cut in various places, and it is also typewritten on the page both horizontally and vertically, as indicated below.]

[horizontal]
today is beautiful and i am dreaming of you and enigma and how we are together today: your words in my ears making [me] limp and taut by turns with delight. oh, i am sure we could use each other today.

i like to believe that you are writing my music now: god knows i'm not doing it, because it simply seems to happen. the prestissimo is incredible the way you are and is perhaps a description and song about you.

banalities: blue check arrived and dv et Helmsley got theirs; i am afflicted with bills of all description, but do not seem to be able to be sensible about money. passed by clyde's yesterday with their socks; they look beautiful. had, for a change, a pleasant time with

---

This letter gives some idea of the breadth of Cage's associations at the time: Schuyler Chapin, American impresario and producer (later president of Lincoln Center and still later general manager of the Metropolitan Opera), Oliver Smith, American set designer, Jerome Robbins, American theater producer, director, and choreographer, and Edwin Denby, the American dance critic who both Cage and Cunningham considered the finest of his time. Cage also references Joseph Campbell, American Professor of Literature at Sarah Lawrence College who gained popular recognition for his work in comparative mythology and religion (and who was married to the Martha Graham Company dancer, Jean Erdman). He mentions the newly-published *A Skeleton*

Schuyler; he informs me that Oliver who called the other day and wanted to know whether you could hold a tune and what kind of voice you had, with Robbins, has you in mind for the lead of their dance-musical; it doesn't mean you have to sing like galli-curci, but like American sailor[s] sing (and see stripes au meme temps?)

there is apparently a part in the book where you would go through a tunnel of love and everyone thinks you would do it very well: so do i, please go through mine, taking your time, if you will.

also schuyler had evening with virgil and v.t. now says i am ultra-genius, having seen some of 2 piano work, and that i am on a par with picasso, schoenberg, stravinsky, satie, matisse, cezanne, van gogh etc. ad nauseum: schuyler now thinks virgil had good reasons for not reviewing other concerts, will blare next one to skies, that his review of it is really already written, that he has been making careful decisions about what to say etc. i don't like being great. it's not good for my relation with calliope, who by the way, is not female, and looks exactly like you.

pardon the intrusion: but when in september will you be back? i would like to measure my breath in relation to the air between us.

Key to Finnegans Wake: Unlocking James Joyce's Masterwork (Harcourt Brace, 1944), co-authored by Campbell and Henry Morton Robinson, which he was reading at the time. In short order Joyce would join Satie as one of Cage's idols. And, lastly, "galli-curci," properly Amelita Galli-Curci, an Italian coloratura soprano whose early-20th-century gramophone records gave rise to her widespread popularity.

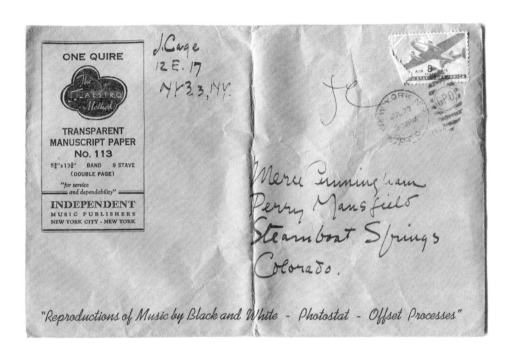

[*vertical*]

in one letter i said absurd things about inexpressivity; obviously wrong, but what i meant was that high expressivity often comes about through no attempt to make it or to express anything. had dinner one night with denby; i think he's a sad little man who's frightened of something. read his poetry which has some good qualities, but is by no means off this earth. i keep reading marvelous myths in joe's book, but joe, too, is not really fine fine writer. of course, this is first draft i have and he will probably improve it. would you like me to send copy of finnegan book which is out now or would you rather save that for home-reading?

need you deliciously.

gas bill came but is nothing; do not worry about it.

prestissimo will be complex at first, then simple then complex and then faster yet to end entire piece which should be finished in two weeks, because have more things to write; i am so happy with this music that i shall be sad when it is all written. each sound has gotten to be friendly and something i know and have pleasure with; they are so well trained, too.

send me some little twig or a hair from near enigma or a piece of grass you touched and sunbathed with, mon prince.

POEM.   CAUSE: I LOVE YOU.

As leaf with tree, I long to be
With you. A twig connection
If no other, would satisfy.

Sap from your trunk to vivify
My tissues; my one election:
On food you give to have satiety.

Will leaf turn dry and dead? My
Deep need to pale affection
Fade? Will snail transform to tree?

If leaf dies, Spring will mystify
The Winter. No death for tree:
Leaf adorned,'twill live in ev'ry
                        section.

[Undated, postmarked July 27, 1944]
12 E. 17th St., New York

[NB: This envelope contains three items: a short poem ("Poem. Cause: I Love You"), a short composition ("Song for Merce"), and a letter]

good news: joyce sent 45 bucks for rent. instead of sending half to you, i'll pay the august rent and we won't have to worry till mid september again. i've also payed the gas and light bill which the change from your 25 dollars payed your share of. bad sentence. so.

     last two days have been dull stumbling block as far as music went. why such things happen i do not know. one is racing along as my letters must have testified and then all of a sudden this thud-like absence of the muse occurs. Perhaps she went to see you. also the heat is something that doesn't remove itself easily from the mind. i have taken to drink. my loneliness is execrable. i have seen so many movies i could choke. i think of you till i'm blue in the face. i love you, monsieur.

Joyce (Wike) has come and gone, sending much-needed money to cover her "rent."

i thought of a line for Miss Mansfield:

A BOAT FOR STEAMBOAT!

A SPRING FOR COLORADO!

The second line is for you.

Where are the four walls? how is the mother? and the father? and the brother and sister? and are the furies well? is America marshall gonna sing that song?

before the muse went away, i wrote first part of second section which goes prestissimo. i haven't heard it yet but f. and g. said they would work on it and call me because it's in difficult-to-play area.

i want more neurotic love-songs. or don't you feel neurotic?

oliver called up and i found out they want you very much and when will you be back they want to know. it's not the lead, however. but it's something you would like, and apparently they don't care now whether you sing or not. you will make lots of money and can back my next concert which is secretly dedicated to you and you could have all the money left over [after] the sale of tickets. only thing I don't like is that robbins is good but you are prince and the prince should do the choreography. but maybe it wouldn't hurt.

do you miss me? maybe you would make a dance for the two piano deal. or maybe the music is too abstract, je ne sais pas. i hope you will like it. maybe you won't at all. every now and then I get frightened because I think you might not like it. but it is written straight. and I would not write it if i didn't love you deep.

SONG FOR MERCE

[Undated, postmarked August 2, 1944]
12 E. 17th St., New York

[typewritten:]
Au prince-dieu, mon amour des montagnes:

today is hot but beautiful; (there was an astonishing thunderstorm with hail which God only knows how he managed to make today.) and i love you.

the flower you sent in last letter brought muse back and now i am glad to report that i have written half of sixth part and can see at least one convincing way of getting through to the very end (7 8 and 9)! i will hear some more wednesday; nowadays i have to leave the music with them because it is too hard to sight-read. Goes too fast (the better to describe you, lightning is used).

7 8 and 9 are short pieces. 6 is long. So you see, it is going to be finished. it will be hard to believe. i have the impression that it is getting better and better as i go along, which will be good if true, since it will help to maintain interest over such a long period. This fast tempo makes the slower one seem dull in retrospect.

Cage reports that he is enthusiastically reading *The Complete Grimm's Fairy Tales*, edited by James Stern, illustrated by Josef Schari, with commentary by Joseph Campbell, likely in the edition that was part of the Pantheon Fairy Tale & Folklore Library, published in 1944. Cage is lonesome, which is expressed somewhat under his breath, but his reference to performing "onanistic orgies" is a dead giveaway. The last paragraph, handwritten, speaks about his dinner conversation with Louis Horst, long-time musical director and composition teacher for Martha Graham's school and company. This section of the letter also makes fleeting reference to Minna Lederman (also known as Minna Daniel), long-time editor of *Modern Music*, a journal that exerted considerable influence over the direction of pre-World War II American music. Their extant correspondence is voluminous, their

But the slow comes first and is by itself very beautiful. i feel i have been lucky and pray i can maintain this thing to the end. Rasa of wonder and tranquility i hope is established.

I finished reading joe's epilogue to the Grimm Fairy tale book, and it is very beautiful. I think it's the finest thing he's written. I may go out to Siasconset to see them and there copy this score, if it is finished in time. Also supposed to go to Amagansett again for a week, but am not too crazy to do so.

the britains downstairs are amazed at how much i work, and i'm a little bit amazed too. I generally get here by 7 or 8, go out for lunch around 2 and come back, staying until 7 8 or 9 or 10 it was last night. i sleep some too, and would sleep here, except that there are mosquitoes during the night. i read your letters over and over and now that i've finished reading joe's manuscripts, i think i'll take to Jung. Except that mostly i just dream about you. Then i get an idea for the music and go put it down. I can't work at the music constantly because it gets dead in my ears, so i rest and then start in again etc. As you know. Britain says i should patent the prepared piano for apartment houses because it doesn't bother them downstairs.

---

lifelong relationship frequently on the brink of ruin for what Lederman felt was Cage's occasional disregard for her feelings. As Edwin Denby once said, Minna was "all love and fury," and she unleashed both on her young friend, who was 16 years her junior.

i want to do everything with you: eat drink sleep talk laugh cry be quiet be touched touch to see you dance and to see you summer-beautiful, —i will have to close my eyes when you come in the room and open them slowly

NEXT DAY: failed to mail supra, so am adding to it, just for the sensation of maybe talking to you. Monsieur, i would like to whisper this (for the fear the notes might erase themselves or be gathered up and blown away by the muse): i have finished the sixth part! Seven minutes of sheer magic. Tempo will now increase to the limits of human ability for the last three short parts.

another beauty letter from you arrived with leaves in it. They are magnificent autumn colors. And i sense a majesty you are making for yourself. Glad 4 walls is going beautifully. it was to be taken for granted that 4 people can't move. Catch perhaps a group of swans. Invoke the muse. 'i liked the Nietszche touch.

It is still hot as hell and muggy as the very devil. However, it is not utterly still, and so one can live. When i get sexy, i do onanistic orgies in your name.

Tonight i have to go and see some lithuanian dances etc sponsored by the l[eague] of composers because i have to review the stillness for m[odern] music. Wish to hell i hadn't said i'd do it. When i finish the last three movements, will go to sunshine and copy them; when you get back it will be 'spiral bound' and neat, and in rehearsal!

[handwritten:]
another day: early morning—stayed up late talking with Lou about music: aesthetic discussion over a bottle of wine; also had dinner with Louis Horst whom I ran into on street. And a long talk with him and saw the pictures he has (the Klee is beautiful); he talked a lot about our concert which he thought was very fine (apparently mellowed in his mind) and he looks forward to seeing next one.

Also about Satie whom he thinks not great composer but great
aesthetician. I am going to take the "Socrate" (which I have now)
over and we'll go through it together. We got along very nicely.
I am still overjoyed about finishing long movement yesterday +
will spend today copying (only flaw being that I have to go to a
l[eague] of composers deal in Brooklyn tonite: went yesterday [to]
Central Pk: bored to tears but duty to Minna Lederman) whereas
wanted to hear fizdale + gold playing yrs. truly. I have never spent
such musical period in life as ever since preparing for concert.
Write music, talk music, think music, etc. Louis thought my music
for your dances excellent because he doesn't remember it, having
seen dances + not remembering being disturbed by music (which
is right).

> I love you.
> J.

[Undated, postmarked August 12, 1944]
12 E. 17th St., New York

Monsieur des Montagnes:

heat wave here again (incredibly hot); no word from you for over a week (you must be busy as hell getting 4 walls finished; i hope it's coming well and that you haven't murdered any neighbors. i had great snag time in my 2 piano music, and anger time with parents and threw away pages of music and am now back in 6th part, and i think doing better, merci fizdale and gold [who] haven't been able to play for a long time what with sickness and house-hunting. apparently nothing to rent in this city.

   would you consider saving a little vacation spirit to spend with me someplace in nature? it looks like i won't get this finished very soon. i had hoped to go and see jean and joe, but can't now. i am trying very hard to keep the imagination alive. janie bowles is here for a few days and i am going to have dinner with her tonite.

   i need you desperately.

Cage makes passing reference here to Jane Bowles (née Auer), an American writer and playwright married to the American composer and novelist, Paul Bowles. While neither Cage nor Cunningham was especially close to either, their paths crossed variously. Bowles would serve in the 1940s as a music critic for the *New York Herald Tribune*, under Virgil Thomson, Cunningham danced (with Jean Erdman and others) in the premiere performance of Bowles's *The Wind Remains* in "The Third Serenade" concert given at the Museum of Modern Art in New York (March 30, 1943), and in 1947 both Cage and Bowles would be contributors to the score for the experimental film by Hans Richter, *Dreams That Money Can Buy*. The Bowles would live most of their

please even lie to me if necessary about coming back, some day to look forward to i need, even if it isn't true.

in case you need any spirit help i am putting all i have with this in envelope. deeply and in the night.

---

lives abroad, with Paul, who became best known as a writer, becoming strongly associated with Tangiers, where he would remain until his death in 1999.

AU ROI D'AMOUR ET DES MONTAGNES:

Your bel-lettre with sound enclosed arrived and placed me
in ecstatic condition induced by many readings. bell goes about
in my pants pocket near the nameless one who misses you violently.

i am getting along somewhat better with the piece: i am about
to copy sixth part and see what it sounds like; i have a few
doubts and some unknown quantities which i think i will leave
because there are possible relations to the spirit involved which
i am not sure of. a title for you:

SERENATA for TWO PIANOS

1.   with grace
     and with ease
     (a distant perhaps)
     i love you.

2.   to leave this earth
     the need the pain the sleep
     the insane forms and again
     even in death

this music is in my sleep and gives me both pleasantnesses and
nightmares. oh, to end it!

Love,

John

104

[Undated, postmarked August. 15, 1944]
12 E. 17th St., New York

AU ROI D'AMOUR ET DES MONTAGNES:

Your bel-lettre with sound enclosed arrived and placed me in
ecstatic condition induced by many readings. bell goes about in
my pants pocket near the nameless one who misses you violently.
    i am getting along somewhat better with the piece: i am
about to copy sixth part and see what it sounds like; i have a few
doubts and some unknown quantities which i think i will leave
because there are possible relations to the spirit involved which i
am not sure of. a title for you:

	SERENATA for TWO PIANOS	
	1.	with grace
Love,		and with ease
John		(a distant perhaps)
		i love you.
	2.	to leave this earth
		the need the pain the sleep
		the insane forms and again
		even in death

this music is in my sleep and gives me both pleasantnesses and
nightmares. oh, to end it!

[Undated, postmarked August 17, 1944]
12 E. 17th St., New York

<u>Monsieur</u>:

Curious problem I have with words (I was not born an Irishman as you): tonight I wd. love to write an essay about music—it seems to me I know some things tonight—but good God! For hours with pencil in hand + only one stupid sentence. Who tied my tongue + stopped the spirit for words?

Maybe I can tell you what vision I have: rhythm is like the air or water or the ether that the planets move in,—it is in fact like space, and the whole problem in writing notes or making movements, etc., is to not destroy it. It has not the slightest thing to do with anything that is put into it: an accent or a metre or what else; it only begs to be free to be.

Does that mean anything?

The other thing I have idea about is tones (pitches): they least kill the spirit when they arrange themselves for the most part in scales or scale-like structures. So used they evoke + are

This is a contemplative letter wherein Cage shares in rather poetic terms his developing ideas about rhythm and pitch. He also makes passing reference to more of what he was reading at the time, which included a special edition of *Kenyon Review* (1944) celebrating the centenary of the English poet and Jesuit priest, Gerard Manley Hopkins (1844–1889). It's interesting to note that this particular issue contains an article by a young Canadian English professor by the name of Marshall McLuhan, titled "The Analogical Mirrors." McLuhan was unknown to Cage at the time and this article goes unnoted, but as an internationally recognized media theorist some 20 years later, author of the phenomenally successful *Understanding Media: The Extensions of Man* (McGraw-Hill, 1964), McLuhan would greatly influence the composer's thinking. Incidentally, Cage's slightly forlorn

magic. If jumps in the scale are used, one must soon reestablish scale or magic is gone, + petty sentiment rules. Proofs by way of example from graved-past. Debussy, Schoenberg, Bach, Mozart, Palestrina, Hindus. I will have to talk about this because I can't sitting alone see all the angles.

I am resting from composing by doing copying (of which have great deal to do); still have 7 minutes to write. I bought a beautiful copy of *Kenyon Review* (Summer issue) which has many articles about G. M. Hopkins in it and a beautiful article about economics + Adams' *Law of Civilization + Decay*.

Great lightning + thunder + rain tried to remove horror-heat but failed.

When are we going to be together?

~~The Nameless One~~

---

remark to Cunningham that he was "not born an Irishman as you" reminds me of something Cage once said, long after he'd composed his beloved *Roaratorio: An Irish Circus on Finnegans Wake* (1979): if he ever suffered a serious accident, said he, and required a transfusion, he hoped that it would happen in Ireland so that he might get a little Irish blood. Not surprisingly, Irishman Cunningham would in 1983 create a *Roaratorio* of his own, which thereafter joined Cage's work on the stage.

[Undated, postmarked August 19, 1944]
12 E. 17th St., New York

Prince:

I gleaned from last letter that you are pleased and fond of 4 walls—nothing could make me happier—also fanatic response from inexperienced ones marvelous. I hope you get pictures, visual or verbal, because I for one want to know clearly what took place which spirit letters do not in any detailed manner divulge.

You say "Are you happy?" I am not miserable because I look to some day when I am with you; otherwise I have to keep fanatically busy for fear of madness of needing you sooner than you will be here. Please don't be pestered by me (let me rave).

2 piano work has been salvation because it is when what part of is closest to you is living. I have finished sixth part after long weeks of work on it. I have some of next part done. Also copied up to date. Tomorrow have dinner with Fizdale + Gold + hear it. I have not heard it for so long 'twill be good. When do you go to Salt Lake? When is performance? You said you were sometimes

The premiere of *Four Walls* is imminent, and Cunningham is pleased. The work is described as a dance-play, written, directed, and choreographed by Cunningham to a score by Cage, which was performed by Drusa Walker. Cage later described it as being full of repetition and written all in "white notes." It's in the key of C, he noted, "and it goes on and on." (As such, it's seen by some as a precursor to the later minimalist pieces of Steve Reich and Philip Glass.) Arch Lauterer was also on the summer faculty at Perry-Mansfield, and he not only provided set and lighting design but was also credited as co-director. From 1933 to 1943, he taught at Bennington College, and from 1943 to 1945 served as head of the theater department at Mills College. Lauterer collaborated with many choreographers, including Graham (*Letter to the World* [1940], *Deaths and Entrances* [1943]), Humphrey,

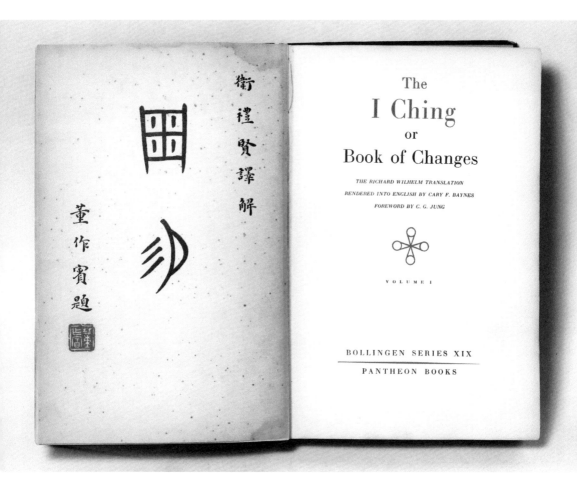

衞禮賢譯解

𣇄

董作賓題

The
I Ching
or
Book of Changes

THE RICHARD WILHELM TRANSLATION
RENDERED INTO ENGLISH BY CARY F. BAYNES
FOREWORD BY C. G. JUNG

V O L U M E I

BOLLINGEN SERIES XIX

PANTHEON BOOKS

feeling in fog between Arin and me. But you must know that every note written for you I feel unworthy.

I know now that you won't say when you're coming back because you are so happy to be in the West; but that some day you will arrive beautifully like a sudden miracle for me. I so deeply hope we can be in beauty place together if only for few days to make a world for dreaming.

Tomorrow I will know whether fifth + sixth parts work as they should. My spirit is tired and I hope they do because I would, I am ashamed to say, have trouble facing great rewriting problems (I have so inch-by-inch struggled). I feel ragged and full of fatigue. Worn as an old shoe. Ready as a ripe fruit for rebirth.

Give my love as you will to the various elements that are you (lavish and long attention to Enigma; open ear to all your words; and thirsty eye and hungry hands and aching limbs and spirit that only jumps and lives for you).

Send me more ways to breathe.

Oh God I am lonely.

Holm, and Weidman. In 1946, his work would be featured in "Stage Design by Arch Lauterer," an exhibition at New York's Museum of Modern Art (August 28–November 3, 1946). As earlier noted, the premiere of *Four Walls* took place on August 22, 1944, at Steamboat Springs, Colorado, and included Cunningham's libretto, "Sweet love, my throat is gurgling." This was the one and only complete performance of this work, which was never again performed in its entirety in Cage or Cunningham's lifetime.

[Undated, postmarked September 1944]
12 E. 17th St., New York

[NB: This letter is both typewritten and handwritten, as indicated]

[typewritten:]
your letters about 4 walls magnificent; would have given eye-teeth and right arm to see it; hope you will give me illustrated lecture about it when here. oh, soon, heart jumps with wondering that moment into existence.

music on its way this afternoon; preparations probably too.

have surprise for you in form of late satie pieces (a suite which is beautiful and very rare (100 copies only)).

both things arrived: suitcase at hudson st. and package here (shall not open until you get here—never liked to be alone when openings go on.)

brittain baby soon; i leave key in hall so doctor may be called at midnight if necessary.

i cannot tell you how happy your summer-successes make me: maybe you know.

A Book of Music is finally finished (and finally titled) and its premiere is imminent! Cage seems pleased, in spite of Lou Harrison's remark to him after hearing the piece in rehearsal that it sounds "dangerously like Stravinsky in parts." Arnold Schoenberg and Igor Stravinsky, the undisputed giants of contemporary composition, were both resident in Los Angeles throughout the 1940s (Schoenberg becoming a U.S. citizen in 1941 and Stravinsky in 1946) and young composers across America felt compelled to take one side or the other. Cage was definitely on the side of Schoenberg, meaning that he was at least implicitly antagonistic toward Stravinsky's work. Cage had studied with Schoenberg in the 1930s and it would be the Austrian composer's radical ideas about atonality that most influenced Cage's early compositional direction.

I HAVE FINISHED MY TWO PIANO MUSIC! And the
curious thing is I am ready to start something else; my feelings
alternate between thinking i have made some beauty, and think
i have failed utterly. I will reserve judgement for you to make.
Actually I won't hear it until you do, because now I have to copy
it on transparent paper which will take approximately 10-14 days
(50 pages) and then send it to printers (another week) and then
to pianists (at least another week): so it is now a thing of the
next month or so as far as ears go. I ran through last movements
yesterday and although i couldn't play the part worth beans
we could see it was alright and has shape. Finale is brilliant as
hell (three minutes of virtuosic passion which expresses itself
in dance-fugal style with gamut runs and tremolandos, chords,
metrical shifts, ostinati, triumphant final subject, unison near
end, faster than ever, and then silent breath with return for
three measures to calm grace of first movement but in form first
movement never gave[ )]. A suite of five solos precedes the finale
which are like jewels or detailed plans for delight: they are in
more than strict classical style. Before that the long sixth part
which i had to work on so long and which now goes gracefully
and miscellaneously to its end. Before that prelude to second
part which is a wow and which also introduces subject of finale.
First and second movements of 2nd part are modeled on first and
second movements of 1st part. God! the form of this thing is so
worked out; i am going to go through for icti now and see whether
they have taken care of themselves when i wasn't looking; if they
come near a shape i shall shape them up exactly with addition
of grace where necessary. By the way, finished piece on Tuesday:
would have written to you then but had no address.

Lou says it is dangerously like Stravinsky in parts, but since
i am not that familiar with Stravinsky it doesn't bother me too
much. Brittain says i now have clear style of my own which he
could recognize even if the piano was unprepared. Enough—must

leave room for heart and talks with you and spirit. Piece will be called simply: *A Book of Music* for 2 pianos. Inside program will be concise statement regarding rhythmic phrase structure written by somebody else.

[handwritten:]
have worn long pencils down to their ends writing this. It is for you.

Must soon get domestic so that house shines when you walk in (wish to hell we had a big bed instead of these little back breakers).

There is beautiful spirit + feeling in studio (when distraught, it calms; when lethargic, it excites; it has been good for work).

Yrs

[Undated, postmarked October 26, 1944]
12 E. 17th St., New York

Dear President

Mail enclosed. Hunter has not said a word yet. I finally finished
copying your work and Ms is out of my hands. Will cost $20.00 for
three copies! I so nearly lost eyesight that I have an appointment
to have eyes examined next Monday—your performance day.
I hope you dance beautifully. I am sorry that I will not see you.
Please capture all hearts present.

    The muse has not settled yet; I hope she is hovering near me,
because I want to start a new piece. This is not a music writing
day; however, to ease conscience I went to library and read book
after book. When I got up it was hard to walk. Do you get to go to
the other Coolidge concerts? Glad the Hindemith is beautiful.

    Miss you
    J.

[Undated, postmarked October 27, 1944)
12 E. 17th St., New York

Heard beautiful talk by Joe on Finnegan last night + saw Barbara
Morgan there. Had expected her to be more giantess than she
is. She says to tell you she had a successful beautiful picture of
Unfocus. You appear twice in picture + she is pleased with it +
wants you to know time not wasted. I am in mood for spirit but
no spirit arrives. Such things are forever secret and a wall against
desire.

Has Martha said that "Appalachian Spring" is from a "Line
by" Hart Crane or is it coincidental?

All day and all yesterday wanting to write and nothing;
something to ward off bitterness needed.

Cage reports having attended Joseph Campbell's talk in
New York on the subject of James Joyce. Campbell was reputedly a marvelous speaker ("a gifted storyteller," "a witty
raconteur"), and his talk surely drew a wide audience. Cage
tells Cunningham that he's finally met Barbara Morgan, an
American photographer who became well known for her de-
pictions of modern dancers, among them a now well-known
photograph of the 21-year-old Cunningham in his leaping
entrance as March in a performance of Graham's *Letter to
the World* (1940). Morgan also captured especially memora-
ble images of Graham herself, as well as Erick Hawkins, José
Limón, Doris Humphrey, and Charles Weidman.

heard beautiful talk by
Joe on Finnegan last night
& saw Barbara Morgan
there. Had expected her
to be more giantess than
she is. She says to
tell you she had a
successful beautiful
picture of Unfocus.
You appear twice in

picture & she is pleased
with it. & wants you
to know time not wasted

I am in mood for spirit
but no spirit arrives. So
things are forever secret as
a wall against desire.
• Has Martha said that
"Appalachian Spring" is from
a line by Hart Crane or is
it coincidence?

All day and all yesterday
wanting to write and
nothing? Something to ward
off bitterness needed

[Undated, postmark illegible but likely 1946]
326 Monroe St., New York

Dearest:

Finally found a shoe place that is willing to make them and that
promises delivery before May 12; it is called La Ray. However, they
need your shoe size width etc. In other words, you must send me
a size that is a number and a letter (like 12E or whatever your foot
is). I just called Katy and got her size number. Send me yours both
in street and ballet terminology. As soon as possible, comme tu
comprends.

I have also mailed the contracts etc.

The suite will be ready Friday which means that I will send it
then to your Cincinnati address (Emery Auditorium). OK?

I have a ghastly amorous problem. I don't know what to do
and that is why I must tell you about it; it is not your problem, it
is mine but perhaps you will be able to write something that will
bring balm. I have nightmares and can't sleep and am in general
nocturnal misery. I am worried that maybe you don't love me

A lot of teeth gnashing and soul searching in this letter, the
date of which reflects a significant gap in Cage's letters to
Cunningham. Is Cage giving more than he gets? Are he and
Cunningham a poor fit? Has Cunningham's ardor waned?
Cage indeed appears to be in the throes of "erotic doubt," as
he puts it, making anguished reference to "Frank" and other
of Cunningham's real or imagined lovers. Laussat, who Cage
places at the center of a parable he's written on the subject of
jealousy that he sees mirroring his own plight, was Cage and
Cunningham's spirited household cat.

and that you will love other misters. I know you love me as artist friend and spirit but I am afraid that it is I who always forces sex; I am in erotic doubt—I know you love freedom. I don't know how much I mean to you as sex or whether you simply tolerate me. I love you and I want to be faithful to you. I don't know whether you want to be faithful to me or whether you would even consider my possessiveness. Nothing is more desirable to me than the feeling of being possessed by you but I don't know whether you like to be possessed by me. All this comes because of Frank whom I take for granted you will see; and my fears of new Franks. I spend hours wondering how you are in bed with someone else. And whether you give more to others than to me. Selfish of me no doubt but then let me tell [a] small story of Laussat. I took Sonya's white kitten down to the river and Laussat was furiously jealous. She nearly killed the poor little cat, and for hours after she growled at me and clawed till now my hands and arms are all scratched and deeply. I had to give the kitten to the people next door. From what you have said to me, I gather that it would not make much difference to you if I slept with other people. The difference it would make to me is this: There is a strength in an unadulterated relation which there is not in the other kind. Please, if you can and will, write to me about this in words that I can understand. I truly need help. I belong to you if you want me. If you don't want me and if all these feelings are a load to your spirit: Say so now if this is my lot so that I can find some other way to live. If I must.

You have been beautiful to me and always are. I have no complaints; I want to know how you feel; for generally you keep your feelings secret. It seems to me that you love me more nowadays. God knows my love for you has grown and grows continually so that it is with me always and in every place my spirit is. The thought of your body near me is heaven.

Please write some message which is true. And do not be afraid to make my life black if it must be black. If you give me brightness as I hope.

John

[handwritten at bottom:]
I don't know what else to say.

[Undated, postmarked March 19, 1946]
326 Monroe St., New York

Dearest

I am at a peculiar kind of stand-still. Inspiration ceased. I have
discarded one of the *Sonatas* and thrown away many sketches. I
have three good ones finished. Of these Maro has chosen two to
play and I will write, God willing, two more that please. Laussat
and I are at odds but still comforts to one another. She does nature
things in the house which doesn't help matters between us. I
think she does it because I do it and it's the first time that she's
been privy to the little room. I think my standstill is due to having
been impressed pretty deeply by Alan's concert, Lou's new book
on Ruggles and dissonant polyphony, and a long conversation
I had with Virgil re expressivity. I do not know exactly where I
stand. So I am still and waiting. I will copy the sonatas I have
and wait a while. I love you forever. I hope my telegram kept bad
previous letter from having bad effect. Your suit is not being sent
till tomorrow because the weather was bad and they could not let

Reference here is to Cage's *Sonatas & Interludes* (1946–1948),
a masterpiece for the prepared piano some 70 minutes in
length, in which Cage expresses in music the permanent
emotions of Indian tradition; also his first composition using
Hindu philosophy as a basis, inspired in part by his reading
of Ananda K. Coomaraswamy (likely *The Dance of Shiva*,
Essays on Indian Art and Culture, and/or *The Transformation
of Nature in Art*). His piano preparations are elaborate: 45
notes, mainly screws and bolts, but also 15 pieces of rub-
ber, four pieces of plastic, six nuts, and one eraser. Maro
Ajemian, to whom the work is dedicated, gave its first partial
performance at New York's Town Hall on April 14, 1946; the
first complete performance was likely given by Cage himself

me have it safely until tomorrow (Monday). I will send key ring and chain then too. When they get around to making the shoes, should they be in colors or simply plain to be dyed? They may not have the colors in suede they said, and you might have trouble matching what colors they do have. What do you advise? I didn't see Genevieve Jones; she was never in when I called; you should perhaps write to her: 5851 Forbes St. Pittsburgh 17 Pennsylvania. I love you.

My class went beautifully and they want it to go on forever they said; I had about eight in it. And they are composing two-minute dances. They gasped at end of class and said nothing like it had ever happened to them before.

It is very hard for me, not being with you. I miss you deeply.

[*handwritten on left bottom*]:
Love I love you.
<u>Mailing suit now</u>.
Books arrived.

---

at Black Mountain College on April 6, 1948, during his and Cunningham's first visit to North Carolina.

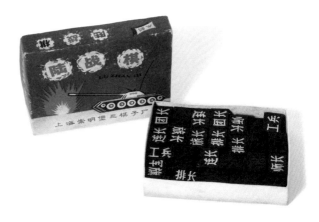

[Undated, postmarked April 2, 1946]
326 Monroe St., New York

Merce my dearest your letter I guess your feet are part of my delight and that is why they didn't seem too big for that color (will try to change it). I think I know my life it is for you—I hadn't heard from you for so long and then your letter written hurriedly and not even with word of love but it puts me in a complete passion. (Would you please lover make love once even though these miles are separating a caress please a night together.)

I am writing a good piece and it is difficult because I don't want to spoil it and the only one I can imagine listening to it is you. I hope when you hear it you will quietly take me deeply in your arms and lengthen the night.

A love letter please in return for mine.

John

Laussat sends her love too.

Throughout these letters, Cage gives intermittent updates on the progress he's making vis-à-vis tasks he's undertaken on Cunningham's behalf. Apartment hunting, paying bills, receiving deliveries, managing repairs to their apartment, forwarding mail. Here we see remarks about the continuing difficulties the two are having with regard to the appropriate size and color of a new pair of shoes Cage is purchasing for Cunningham. (Cunningham loved shoes, and rumor has it that he once went without eating for several days so that he could afford to buy a particularly glamorous pair he'd spotted in a shop window.)

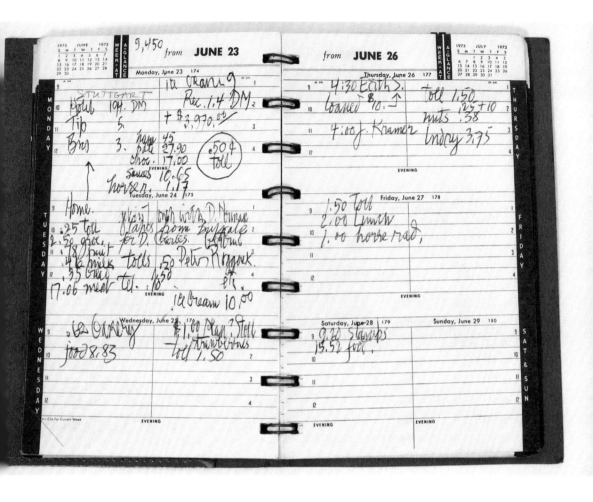

9,450 *from* **JUNE 23**

from **JUNE 26**

Monday, June 23 174

STUTTGART   ice Cream g
Hotel   104. DM   Rec. 1.4 DM
Tip   5.   + $3,970.00
Brkf   3.   Napk .43   (.50 ¢
              Pate 23.90   Toll)
              Choc. 17.00
              sauces 10.65
Horren. 1.17

Tuesday, June 24 175

Home.   Ship 1 box with D. Kramer
.25 Toll   plates from Buffalo
2.50 groc.   for D. Charles. Capitol
.48 mitt   tools .50 Peter Roggock.
.35 Chez   tel. 18.50   et.
17.06 meat   ice Cream 10.00

Wednesday, June 25 176

.62 Carkry $1.00 Play 3 Stell
food 8.83   food strawberries
                Toll 1.50

Thursday, June 26 177

4:30 Earths.
loaned $10.   Toll 1.50
                             .25 + 10
7:00 J. Kramer   nuts .38
                 lndry 3.75

Friday, June 27 178

1.50 Toll
2.00 Lunch
1.00 horse rad,

Saturday, June 28 179   **Sunday, June 29** 180

9.20 stamps
15.52 food.

[on a separate sheet:]

I went to shoe place just now but the man who's making yours is sick today. I left a note about color. Will go back tomorrow.

      Love,

[Undated, postmarked August 19, 1946]
326 Monroe St., New York

[This letter is written on the backside of a program: "Genevieve Jones Presents Merce Cunningham" (Pittsburgh Playhouse, 222 Craft Ave., June 25, 1946, 8:30 P.M.)]

Thank you for letter and nature element. I hope you reach Morris and that your work is going well and stomach revives et al.

I washed my rugs in bathtub (took 2 days). They are finally dry and look cleaner. I finished second piece for orchestra and am searching for the 3rd one. The lily shot up a foot and ½ + bloomed fragrantly.

As soon as you flew away the weather became really heavy + there have been a series of impromptu storms. I see Lou + Minna L. Gita Sarabhai.

Still reading Coomar. + trying to digest. I know definitely, however, that I cannot give up writing music. Saw Alan H[ovhaness] (his Opera is Oct. 11) etc. Beginning rehearsals for concert soon.

Cage references the various people he's been seeing, which included Gita Sarabhai, an Indian musician who had traveled to the U.S. for study. Cage taught her counterpoint, while she informed him on the subjects of Indian music and philosophy. Cage had earlier heard Nancy Wilson Ross speak on the subject of Eastern religions while in the Northwest, her talk, entitled "The Symbols of Modern Art," given at the Cornish School on the occasion of the opening of a Paul Klee exhibit. Ross had influence, but it was from Sarabhai that Cage would learn that in Indian thought the purpose of music is "to sober and quiet the mind, thus making it susceptible to divine influences," which Cage would repeat for decades. While both Cage and Cunningham would in time befriend the entire Sarabhai family (founders of the Sarabhai Textile Mills in Ahmedebad, they would host the Merce

GENEVIEVE JONES PRESENTS
MERCE CUNNINGHAM
PROGRAM OF DANCES

triple-paced	**1**
root of an unfocus	**2**
idyllic song	**3**
tossed as it is untroubled externalization of a laugh within the mind	**4**
	intermission
invocation to vahakn ancient armenian god-king	**5**
experiences	**6**
the unavailable memory of	**7**
totem ancestor	**8**
spontaneous earth	**9**

MUSIC: JOHN CAGE. THE ACCOMPANIMENT FOR 'IDYLLIC SONG' AN ARRANGEMENT OF THE FIRST MOVEMENT OF ERIK SATIE'S 'SOCRATE' (PERMISSION GRANTED BY LA SIRENE MUSICALE, PARIS, AND ELKAN-VOGEL CO., INC., PHILADELPHIA, PA., COPYRIGHT OWNERS). THE MUSIC FOR 'INVOCATION TO VAHAKN' COMPOSED BY ALAN HOVHANESS. THE MUSIC FOR THE SECOND PART OF 'EXPERIENCES' COMPOSED BY LIVINGSTON GEARHART. PIANISTS: JOHN CAGE AND HENRY MAZER. THE COSTUME FOR 'TOTEM ANCESTOR' DESIGNED BY CHARLOTTE TROWBRIDGE. COSTUMES EXECUTED BY ELISABETH PARSONS, AND BY IRVING EISENSTOT. PITTSBURGH PLAYHOUSE, 222 CRAFT AVE., JUNE 25, 1946, 8:30 P.M.

Thank you for letter and nature element. I hope you reach Morris and that your work is going well and stomach revives et al.

I washed my rugs in bath (took 2 days) they are finally dry and look cleaner. I finished second piece for orchestra and am searching for the 3rd one. The lily shot up a foot + ½ + bloomed fragrantly.

As soon as you flew away the weather became really heavy + there have been a series of impotent storms. I see Lou + Mining L. City Garathni.

Still peachy Cooman, I trying to digest. I know definitely, however, that I cannot give up writing music. Saw Alan H. etc Beginning rehearsals for concert soon. His Opera is Oct 11.

remembering is asking : What is the Use? of art? work of life. Discover Answer.

/ Emerson. a Dis couvrons a Dis couvrez Answers. Necessity now to Discover Answers. is

[written along the left and right margins:]
everybody is asking: What is the Use? of art of work of life. Discover Answer. is Necessity now to Discover Answer. Dís fou jours à l'Enigme.

Cunningham Dance Company's first trip to India during its 1964 world tour), Cage remained especially close to Gita and her sister, Gira. Decades later, in the late 1980s, I would have the pleasure of meeting Manorama Sarabhai, a member by marriage of the Sarabhai family, who was visiting her son and daughter-in-law in Long Island. This visit was preceded by one to Dorothy Norman, the American photographer, arts patron, and social activist, who was also resident in Long Island. Cage and I paddled around together in Norman's swimming pool while she napped, the concrete crumbling slightly and the walls surrounding the garden almost entirely covered with hanging vines. Cage wore only cut-off jeans, his body very white due to prolonged lack of exposure to the sun.

[Undated, postmarked August 27, 1946]
326 Monroe St., New York

The phonograph comes to circa $150. Nothing re linoleum yet. Laussat perpetrated fleas + L. Brown threatens poison. I am getting exterminator so that you may live unbitten.

My 3 pieces for orchestra look like they will be 2 instead of 3. Since manner of ending 2nd piece seems to resist too naturally any further sounds. Am becoming more + more interested in not blemishing silence with sound.

It will be new to see you.

Connie has apparently gone stark mad. I hear she is planning to visit you. She borrows money to enable her to carry on creatively in taxis + trains with lg. crayons. She tells that we are her inspiration, malheureuse.

Much scientific work. Bonnie Bird. Hindu thoughts. Maritain (not so good as Coomaraswamy but related). Geeta Sarabhai + Lou. Some Movies. Sarah's back + my class begins next week.

This letter contains Cage's only reference to Bonnie Bird, an American teacher and dancer and Cage's colleague at the Cornish School, where she served as head of the dance department. Bird was a Martha Graham protégé, and she numbered among her students not only Cunningham but also Remy Charlip, who would become a founding member of the Merce Cunningham Dance Company at its formation at Black Mountain College in 1953. While a student at the Cornish School, Cunningham would perform frequently in programs given by Bird's "Cornish Dancers," which in late 1938 into early 1939 began to include dances choreographed by Cunningham himself, including *Unbalanced March*, a solo, and *Jazz Epigram*, a duet.

Stock up in spirit je t'en prie. I will need to borrow some. Let me know time of return so that I can clean away chemicals.

J.

[Undated, no postage, likely hand-delivered]
[Location not indicated]

[NB: The envelope, addressed to only "Merce Cunningham," contains two letters, one handwritten (in French) and one typewritten (in English); these appear in this order below. Undated, but likely c. 1946]

Thank you

Merci, Prince pour tout l'hospitalité chez toi; c'était un vrai joi. Je vais chez moi maintenant parce que je crois que tu aimeras ça meiux. Je laisserai la porte ouverte ainsi que tu pourras toujours entrer si tu veux. Pardonnez mes diables s'il y en a qui restent encore ici. Je les puvirai quand je suis seul. Et j'espère que tu aimes mes anges comme j'aime tou esprit + toi.

   Oh, mon Dieu, ou est les Muses?

      Jean

These are sad letters, both contained in a single envelope. Cage resorts to French in one, wherein he says goodbye to both Merce and the apartment they've shared, and in the other, in English, he reflects on what may have been his role in what he believes is the end of their relationship. Without benefit of Cunningham's letters, it is impossible to tell whether Cage's assessment of things was real or imagined. Further, it is not entirely certain that these two letters date from 1946, since they are in their originals undated. (And given that there are no extant letters from 1945, they may well have been written in late 1944 or even in 1945, reflecting or perhaps even causing something of a year-long

Thank you

Merci, Prince
pour tout l'hospitalité chez
Toi ; c'était un vrai joi.
Je vais chez moi maintenant
parce que je crois que tu
aimeras ça mieux. Je
laisserai la porte ouverte
ainsi que tu pourras
toujours entrer si tu veux.
Pardonnez mes diables

S'il y en a qui restent
encore ici. Je les
punirai quand je
suis seul. Et j'espère
que tu aimes mes
anges comme j'aime
ton esprit + toi.
Oh, mon Dieu, où est
les Muses?

Jean

[Translation]

Thank you, Prince, for all the hospitality at your place; it was a real joy. I am going home now because I believe you'll like it better. I shall leave the door open so that you can always come in if you want to.

Forgive my demons if there still remain any here. I shall punish them when I am alone. And I hope that you love my angels the way I love your spirit & you.

Oh, my God, where are the Muses?

Jean

---

hiatus in their correspondence.) In any case, hindsight is all here. History tells us that this relationship was not ending but in its very beginnings, and that it would last for decades to come.

Dearest Merce:

That it would ever end, I never suspected, or could have believed. Your hating me is enough, I suppose. God knows what I will do with that and these feelings of love. No room is small enough for me to lie in.

You are probably safe to remain so strong within yourself and so free of love which brings no mirth but only pain. Whether that way of being was yours naturally or instilled is of little matter.

I have never been so happy as when loving you, yet never so blind and selfish.

I think I have given myself away to you. I don't know what is left. When you began to be indifferent, I took delight in that; when cruel, in that, too. I could have gone on forever, living in a complementary way to your treatment. What now but to get quiet and dead?

Take this as the key which locks me up and frees you from me. How long I can be in my little space with your spirit, or whether it will stay with me, I don't know.

Perhaps a prayer for sleep.

Dearest Merce:

That it would ever end, I never suspected, or could have believed. Your hating me is enough, I suppose. God knows what I will do with that and these feelings of love. No room is small enough for me to lie in.

You are probably safe to remain so strong within yourself and so free of love which brings no mirth but only pain. Whether that way of being was yours naturally or instilled is of little matter.

I have never been so happy as when loving you, yet never so blind and selfish.

I think I have given myself away to you. I don't know what is left. When you began to be indifferent, I took delight in that; when cruel, in that, too. I could have gone on forever, living in a complementary way to your treatment. What now but to get quiet and dead?

Take this as the key which locks me up and frees you from me. How long I can be in my little space with your spirit, or whether it will stay with me, I don't know.

Perhaps a prayer for sleep

Some 40 Years Later by Laura Kuhn

By the time I entered John Cage's life, in the mid-1980s, he and Merce Cunningham had been together for more than 40 years. Rhythms in the loft they shared at 101 W. 18th St. in New York City had naturally been established, which always revolved around work, entertaining, intermittent interviews and visits by researching scholars and performers, and frequent, sometimes lengthy tours. Cage had all but stopped traveling with the Merce Cunningham Dance Company as one of its musicians, in part because of the increasing demands of his own schedule but also because he was running out of steam. He continued his duties without complaint as one of the company's chief spokespersons and fundraisers, however, and he was constantly being called upon to reach out to someone for money or to write a letter or design a program for this or that fundraising effort. The idea of a vacation was never once mentioned, and a trip to the local cinema was a rare and special occasion. (I only remember them going to see two films—*Dreamchild* [1985, starring Coral Browne and Ian Holm], and *Imagine* [1988, an intimate documentary on John Lennon]—both of which they greatly enjoyed.)

The first day I formally met John Cage at his 18th St. loft, he met me at the elevator. I later learned that he did this with all visitors, welcoming them into the home he had shared with Merce Cunningham for nearly a decade. He was amiable but preoccupied, and I soon learned why: it was window-washing day, and the seemingly endless number of plants that lined the windowsills on the east and south walls of the apartment had to be removed to the floor. Meanwhile, the entire apartment smelled of granola, which was baking merrily in the oven. Together we proceeded to move the plants—blooming cultivars, cacti and succulents, evergreens of many kinds—while getting acquainted. Cage learned that I was near the end of a New York City residency in between graduate degrees at UCLA, and I learned that he was unnervingly behind on his work on *Europeras 1 & 2*, a commission from the Frankfurt Opera. The world premiere was scheduled to take place in roughly six months, and he was nowhere near finished. Cage had taken on a "Wagnerian" role, assuming full charge of every aspect of the composition and its production—music, of course, for both orchestra and singers, but also casting, lighting, costumes, stage design and actions, and even the program booklet. He and Andrew Culver, his able computer programmer, were that day in the thick of designing the lighting program. At the end of what had been an informal interview, Cage invited me to work with him and Culver, and I answered with a resounding "Yes!" I snagged an area yet untouched, the costumes, and, at Cage's suggestion, also agreed to help wherever extra hands and eyes were needed, creating actions for the performers, proofreading orchestral parts, and the like. From the start we both knew we were well suited, for a variety of reasons, but perhaps mostly because Cage didn't like to tell people what to do, and I, a cheeky graduate student, believed I could do anything. And that was music to his ears.

I would arrive for work each day after Merce left for his Westbeth studio, around 10 am, and stay until 5 pm, when John would usually unwind from the day's work by having a glass of wine and playing a game or two of chess with his good friend, the artist Bill Anastasi. Anastasi had to leave by 6:30 pm, at which time Merce would return from the studio and usually regale John with

a recapitulation of the most exasperating moments of his day, followed by a bath in the big jacuzzi tub that they'd installed in the larger of the loft's two bathrooms. While Merce bathed, John would put in a call to the Cunningham Dance Foundation office, taking a moment away from the preparation of dinner to chastise whoever was in charge for their behavior that day. More often than not, John had invited guests to dinner, much to Merce's displeasure, and in the rare instances when the two had privacy for the evening they'd eat together, and then John would continue working while Merce retired to the small back room that doubled as an office to watch a bit of TV. (I was never there to actually see this, but I still laugh when remembering how the small, yellow couch in that room was positioned not toward the television, but toward the south window and thus down 6th Avenue, with a clear view of the Twin Towers of the World Trade Center. I also couldn't imagine Merce ever being really comfortable in there, given that he was at least a foot taller than the couch was long.)

John and Merce almost always had a cat. When I arrived, it was Skookum, a sultry-eyed, demure black female, her name derived from Chinook Jargon. (Cunningham's 1936 high-school yearbook, which he served as assistant editor, was named the *Skookum Wa Wa*.) With Skookum's mysterious disappearance a year or so later, Losa joined the household, a gift from the poet Sean Bronzell. Losa (fully, Losa Taxicab Rinpoche) was also black, but a wild and feisty male. He wasn't shy and he loved the camera, brazenly insinuating himself into photo shoots taking place at the loft without a moment's notice. He also didn't hesitate to claw or bite anyone he found even mildly irritating, and after Cage's death he took up the annoying habit of lying in wait in the mornings and then mercilessly attacking Merce's ankles as he hobbled to the bathroom in his bare feet. Years later, on the morning after Cage's death, Merce received the gift of an abandoned kitten from Julie Lazar, then curator at the Museum of Contemporary Art in Los Angeles who was working to complete Cage's *Rolywholyover A Circus*. She'd named him Enso, inspired by the hand-drawn circles of uninhibited brushstrokes in Zen practice, but Merce quickly renamed him Blotch. Unlike Losa, Blotch was timid, quiet, and sweet, and the two rarely got along.

John took care of the household. He was an excellent cook and by this time he'd fully adopted the macrobiotic diet, which had greatly alleviated the symptoms of his severe arthritis. He seemed to enjoy cooking every bit as much as he loved to compose. He also "made" his own water, a handy distiller always humming away on the kitchen counter, and he was an enthusiastic home gardener who cared for the literally hundreds of plants that were positioned around the loft. (I early on told him that I found his plants beautiful, and he responded by telling me that the secret to the success of any gardener is knowing when to pick off the brown parts.) He was extremely rigid about his diet, but in cooking (as in life) he also was experimental, as evidenced by the lunches he would make for us each day. These were never boring. Mid-day meals could be, at one extreme, a kind of hearty farmer's lunch of beans, rice, steamed greens, and baked sweet potato with a dollop of hummus. At the other, something that might be offered on a California new-age restaurant menu, like miniature tempeh tacos with corn tortillas replaced by sheets of gently toasted nori. On those rare occasions when John was on his own for lunch, he might satisfy himself with just a piece of whole grain bread and a glass of soy milk, which allowed him to return more quickly to work.

The complement of beans and brown rice forms a complete protein and is the foundation of the macrobiotic diet. Merce, however, always insisted upon having a little fish or chicken in addition, and John happily complied. Both John and Merce attributed good health to a good diet, and both found eating healthily while on tour something of a challenge. Merce traveled with cooking paraphernalia for use in hotel rooms (e.g. a rice steamer, an electric kettle, utensils), while John sought out local restaurants that would suffice or else relied on the kindness of presenters who might have a sympathetic mother who would prepare meals to his specifications. When at home in New York, attending this function or that, Cage became known as the guest who brought his own food, which he'd prepare in advance and carry in a well-worn straw basket and which the hostess would then carefully plate and serve. This was also true for both men when traveling on airplanes, much to the bemusement of the flight attendants, especially in first class.

John's stubbornness about maintaining his diet under any circumstances could be problematic. Once, upon his return home

from a trip to Leningrad in 1988 where he'd attended the Third International Music Festival in the USSR, he was shockingly thin and his complexion grey. He explained in a kind of mild hysteria that there was simply nothing to eat ("absolutely everything was cooked in chicken fat!"), so he'd subsisted for 10 days on little more than vodka and the wild greens he'd foraged with local anarchists. It took weeks for the rose in his cheeks to return.

And on one trip we took together to Perugia in 1992 for the Quaderni Perugini di Musica Contemporanea's "John Cage Symposium," he had me scout around for a reputable vegetarian couscous restaurant at which we could take our evening meal each and every day. Being equally reliant upon couscous, once a suitable

establishment was identified, Merce would similarly eat the same meal in the same restaurant night after night when touring. It was sometimes a struggle to find him a dining partner, since most of the company members much preferred to sample a variety of local foods.

Not everyone was enthusiastic about Cage's adoption of the macrobiotic diet and the transition wasn't easy. John himself admitted that at the start of the diet he'd gone into shock at the idea of never again cooking with butter. Merce confided that he'd found pretty much everything that came out of the kitchen in those early days tasteless, and that he often had to feign pleasure to bolster John's confidence. When I first met David Vaughan, archivist of the Cunningham Dance Foundation who'd been around both men for decades, I encouraged him to join us for lunch at the loft, saying "Cage is a marvelous macrobiotic cook!" David simply rolled his eyes and sighed heavily. "Oh, Laura, you never had his Coq au vin," he said, his eyes glazing over. No, things had not always been so austere in the Cage-Cunningham kitchen. John himself told me how he and John Lennon, a neighbor in the West Village apartment building where they both had lived, once consumed an entire pot of crème brûlée that Cage was preparing for a dinner party that night. (Lennon couldn't stay for dinner, so Cage had simply served him the not-quite-finished dessert first.) Cage definitely had a sweet tooth, and years later he was particularly excited by the acquisition of an expensive electric ice cream maker, which he loved so much he bought a spare just in case the first one ever stopped working. He didn't use the recipe that came with the machine, of course, which called for mostly cream and sugar, but rather filled the machine's mixing bowl with a concoction of soy milk, bananas, tofu, and Cafix. It was delicious! John generously had one sent to everyone close to him, me and his manager at Performing Artservices, Mimi Johnson, among them.

I didn't begin to really know Merce until after John's death. (Although, once, years earlier, John encouraged Merce to show me something of his work on the computer, which was in the early days of Cunningham's use of Life Forms, a computer software program adaptable to on-screen choreography. He did, and I felt inspired and truly privileged.) They were publicly very private people, and one particular story evidences this nicely. It took place at the end of a post-performance Q & A onstage in Berkeley, California, when questions from the audience were encouraged. One particularly cranky journalist raised his hand. "All right, you two, why don't you tell us about the nature of your relationship?" John and Merce just looked at each other for a few moments, the room holding its breath, their faces without expression. Cage finally said, "Well, I do the cooking and Mr. Cunningham does the dishes." Most people in the audience understood their relationship to be romantic, and the room exploded in laughter.

Neither Cage nor Cunningham was always easy to work with. Merce could be taciturn, secretive, and moody at times, and often gave difficult tasks having to do with his dancers (announcing casting decisions and the like) to others. Even poor John was called upon with uncomfortable frequency to straighten out messes and misunderstandings on Merce's behalf. But, when Merce was happy, everyone was happy. Certainly, any time I heard him whistle around the house (which he did beautifully), I'd smile, since this usually meant he was feeling momentarily light of heart. Cage was intense and demanding and had a tireless work ethic which he expected others to match. I remember one particularly steamy summer day (in a loft without air conditioning), so hot that my computer simply stopped working at least once an hour. After lunch I told John I was going outside for a walk around the block. "What do you mean?!" he asked, incredulous. The very idea that I might be in need of fresh air and of stretching my legs was beyond his comprehension. He would become particularly grumpy when

one of Andrew Culver's computer software programs, developed specifically for Cage's work, was misbehaving. Culver would just smile, unruffled by the news, since such occurrences were natural when working with technology. John, on the other hand, felt as if he'd been taken hostage by a computer bug, since he knew full well that his work would be stalled until Andy was able to identify and fix whatever problem was happening in the code.

And for all of John's wisdom, he could be surprisingly naïve about the world. He didn't watch television or listen to the radio, he didn't follow the stock market or politics, and he didn't vote. In short, he was oddly disconnected from the kind of information known to most everyone around him. When we were working

together on the mesostics for his "Harvard Lectures" (published as *I-VI*, Harvard University Press, 1991), for example, a late addition to the source mix was chance-determined newspaper clippings, an idea Merce proposed after hearing John practice his texts aloud at home. "Might this be a way of bringing in something contemporary?" he asked. So, my job each morning for a few weeks was to throw dice to determine which newspaper(s) to buy and then bring to work. John would then chance determine which article(s) in which paper(s) to include. One morning upon my arrival I discovered him already at work at his small, round table, laughing. "What's up?" I asked. "Did you know that Jessie Jackson is black?!" he exclaimed. A similar exchange took place around his learning of the existence of "crack babies." He was near tears at this news and not much good for the rest of the day.

Cage's death was sudden, although not entirely unexpected, and Merce felt very much alone. I moved in with him for a few weeks to ease the transition and to answer the phone, which rang incessantly for days on end. Many friends came to visit, some ringing the bell and coming upstairs, others quietly leaving flowers in the vestibule of the building. Merce talked more to me in the first few days after Cage's death than he had in six years. He would return the very next day to the studio, but I remember vividly his behavior on that first evening, in the hours just after Cage died. He was distraught, contemplating a life without activity in the house. "What do you mean?" I asked, putting food and drinks out for what would soon be a parade of guests. He said that he would miss the conversation, which was always "so interesting," and that he feared that he would now be completely alone. People came to the loft for Cage, he said, not for him. "Who will want to visit now?"

And then he did an amazingly sweet thing. Cage had been pestering him for months to repair the lid to the clothes hamper, a large, rattan container whose lid was coming to pieces. (Why he didn't simply go out and buy a new one was beyond me.) Cunningham would ignore this and many other of Cage's requests for help around the house and then Cage would brood. But something about this particular appeal had obviously lingered in his mind. He shuffled over to the washer/dryer area that night and retrieved the hamper. He then sat down at the small breakfast table and meticulously taped every loose bit of rattan on that lid, patting it back into place on the basket, all the while smiling wistfully.

The objects that appear in thumbnail images scattered throughout the letters section of this book represent a random sampling of the many items left behind in the Cage/Cunningham household at the time of Merce Cunningham's death in 2009. Most of what John Cage had amassed by way of photographs, books, manuscripts, and documents had long been housed at the John Cage Trust, founded shortly after his own death in 1992, but a single bookcase and several shelves situated around their shared 18th St. loft still held a few special items. Thus, their lives at home, as at work, remained always just a little bit intertwined.

Many things will be at least generally recognizable to most readers: cookbooks and kitchen implements, games, puzzles, and dice, appointment books, a music box, childhood Christmas ornaments, musical instruments, chess pieces, a transistor radio, and tiny little inking brushes. But other things will be really familiar to only a few: Cage's mushrooming basket (p. 44), Cunningham's favorite tiger (p. 67, a gift from Jasper Johns), a clay flower vase (p. 124, handmade by M.C. Richards), Cage's copy of the *I Ching* (p. 109, a gift from Christian Wolff), the wool blanket that often covered their horse-hair mattress sofa, and Cage's chess clock (p. 31). And note one of Tom Marioni's gifts to Cage (p. 26): #86/100 from a limited edition of *Café Society Beer* (1979), specially produced and bottled by Anchor Steam in San Francisco. The label was engraved by Marioni and printed at Crown Point Press, where from 1978 Cage made etchings and prints annually with his close friend, Kathan Brown.

PHOTOGRAPHY CREDITS

This book commemorates the Merce Cunningham Centennial (1919–2019). It is a gift from Laura Kuhn and the John Cage Trust, which Kuhn has directed since its founding in 1993 and which Cunningham served as a member of its board of directors until his death. Cunningham continues to grace our lives through our memories and through his extraordinary works, which live on thanks to the tireless efforts of his new and former dancers and the Merce Cunningham Trust.

Special thanks to:

Ralph Benko
Monique Fong
Emily Sena Martin
Deborah Solomon